Abducting a General

Abducting a General

The Kreipe Operation and SOE in Crete

PATRICK LEIGH FERMOR

JOHN MURRAY

First published in Great Britain in 2014 by John Murray (Publishers)
An Hachette UK Company

1

Main text © The Estate of Patrick Leigh Fermor 2014
Foreword and notes © Roderick Bailey 2014
Guide to the Abduction Route © Chris and Peter White 2014

The moral right of the Authors has been asserted in accordance with the
Copyright, Designs and Patents Act 1988.

Maps drawn by Rodney Paull

A CIP catalogue record for this title is available from the British Library

Hardback ISBN 978-1-444-79658-2
Trade paperback ISBN 978-1-444-79988-0
Ebook ISBN 978-1-444-79659-9

Typeset in Bembo MT Pro by Palimpsest Book Production Ltd, Falkirk, Stirlingshire
Printed and bound by Clays Ltd, St Ives plc

John Murray policy is to use papers that are natural, renewable and recyclable products and
made from wood grown in sustainable forests. The logging and manufacturing processes are
expected to conform to the environmental regulations of the country of origin.

John Murray (Publishers)
338 Euston Road
London NW1 3BH

www.johnmurray.co.uk

Contents

Maps

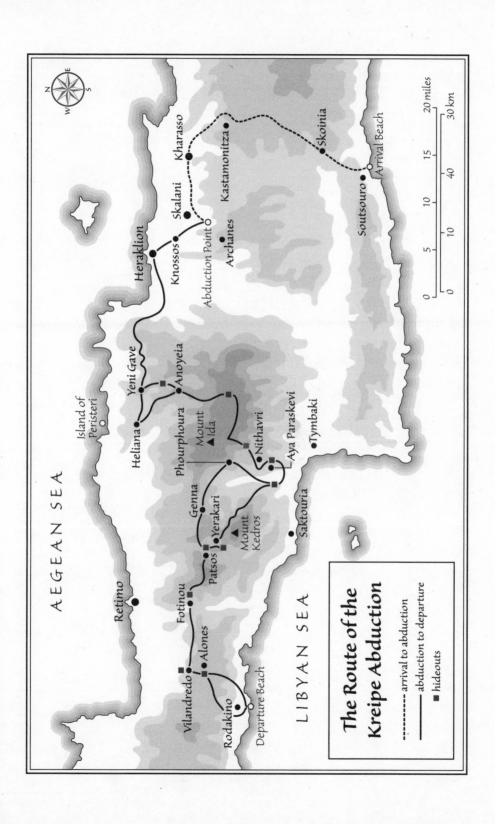

AEGEAN SEA

Island of
Peristeri

Retimo

LIBYAN SEA

Heraklion
Knossos
Skalani
Kharasso
Kastamonitza
Abduction Point
Archanes
Skoinia
Soutsouro
Arrival Beach

Yeni Gave
Anoyeia
Heliana
Phourphoura
Mount Ida
Nithavri
Aya Paraskevi
Tymbaki

Genna
Yerakari
Mount Kedros
Saktouria

Patsos
Fotinou
Alones
Vilandredo
Rodakino
Departure Beach

The Route of the
Kreipe Abduction

.... arrival to abduction
———— abduction to departure
■ hideouts

0   5   10   15   20 miles
0   10   20   30   40   30 km

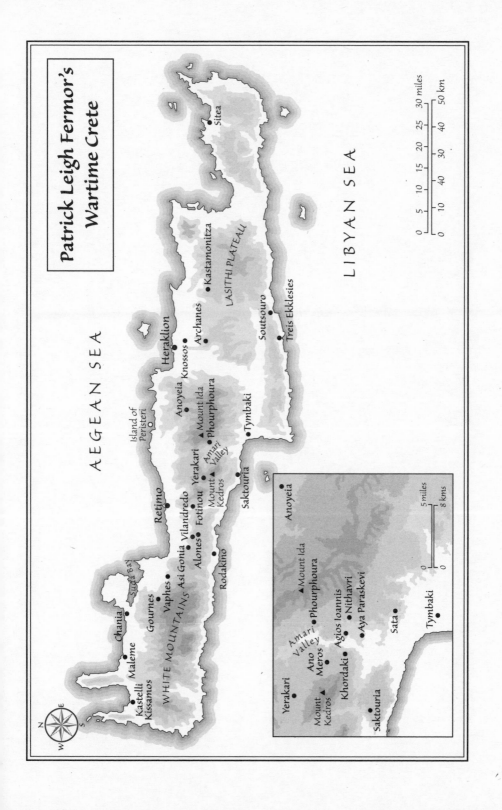

Patrick Leigh Fermor's *Wartime Crete*

AEGEAN SEA

LIBYAN SEA

Chania
Maleme
Kastelli
Kissamos
Suda Bay
Gournes
Vaphes
WHITE MOUNTAINS
Asi Gonia
Vilandredo
Alones
Fotinou
Mount Kedros
Rodakino
Retimo
Yerakari
Amari Valley
Saktouria
Island of Peristeri
Anoyeia
Mount Ida
Phourphoura
Tymbaki
Heraklion
Knossos
Archanes
Kastamonitza
LASITHI PLATEAU
Soutsouro
Treis Ekklesies
Sitea

30 miles
50 km
0 5 10 15 20 25 30 miles
0 10 40 30 40 50 km

Inset map:

Anoyeia
Mount Ida
Phourphoura
Agios Ioannis
Nithavri
Aya Paraskevi
Amari Valley
Ano Meros
Khordaki
Yerakari
Mount Kedros
Saktouria
Sata
Tymbaki

0 5 miles
0 8 kms

Foreword

Knossos, the largest archaeological site on the Mediterranean island of Crete, was the mythical home of King Minos. It was also home, it is said, to the Labyrinth, the maze-like structure that held the Minotaur. Half man, half bull, this creature, which had been devouring a regular tribute of Athenian youths, was finally killed by the Greek hero Theseus with the aid of Ariadne, Minos' daughter: to help his escape, Ariadne gave Theseus a life-saving thread to play out during his descent and lead him to safety when the deed was done. Today, a stone's throw from Knossos sits a pale-bricked property built in the early 1900s by Sir Arthur Evans, a British archaeologist who had pioneered excavations nearby. Quiet, airy, shadowed by trees and shrubs, the house had been Evans's home. It is still called the Villa Ariadne.

In the spring of 1944, at the height of the Second World War, with Evans long gone and Crete under German occupation, the Villa Ariadne was the requisitioned residence of the commander of the garrison's principal division. The forty-eight-year-old son of a pastor, Generalmajor Heinrich Kreipe was a career soldier who had served in the German Army since 1914. During the First World War he had fought on the Western Front as well as against the Russians, been wounded and won two Iron Crosses. Between the wars he had risen in rank to lieutenant colonel. In 1940 he had fought in France as commander of the 209th Infantry Regiment. The following year he had led his men to the oustskirts of Leningrad and won the Knight's Cross, the highest decoration in Nazi Germany for battlefield bravery and leadership. Promotion to general and command of his first infantry division – the 79th – had come in 1943.

Kreipe had been posted to Crete, to command the Wehrmacht's 22nd Airlanding Infantry Division, in early 1944. He had been on the island a matter of weeks when, late one April evening, he left his headquarters in the hillside village of Archanes and, sitting in his chauffeured staff car, began the short, unescorted drive back to Knossos and the Villa Ariadne. A few minutes into the journey, at a lonely junction on the road ahead, red lamps loomed suddenly out of the dark. Kreipe's car was waved to a halt. Lit by the headlights, two figures in German uniform approached . . .

What happened next – and the relentless drama of subsequent days – was later immortalised on screen in *Ill Met By Moonlight*, a 1957 war film produced by Emeric Pressburger and Michael Powell. The film was based on a book of the same name by William Stanley Moss.★ In 1944, 'Billy' Moss – as friends knew him – had been one of a pair of British army officers working clandestinely in Crete who, with a small party of Cretan guerrillas, carried out Kreipe's abduction. *Time* magazine, reviewing Moss's fast-paced account of the action, called it one of the most 'audacious' of the war.†

Moss, twenty-two years old in 1944, had been the junior of the two British officers. A captain in the Coldstream Guards, he had been put ashore on Crete less than a fortnight before. Though hardened by front-line fighting in North Africa, he had never, until that moment, set foot on enemy territory. He knew little of Crete or Cretans. He spoke no Greek. But the skills and experience of Moss's friend and colleague – whose role in the film would be taken by the actor Dirk Bogarde – were quite different.

This officer, a major in the Intelligence Corps, twenty-nine at

---

★ W. Stanley Moss, *Ill Met By Moonlight* (London: Harrap & Co., 1950). A reprint by the Folio Society in 2001 included a fresh afterword by Leigh Fermor. For more on Moss, his life and his wider wartime service, see his subsequent memoir, *A War of Shadows* (London: Boardman, 1952), reprinted by Bene Factum in 2014 with a new introduction by Moss's daughter, Gabriella Bullock, and a brief biographical essay by Alan Ogden.
† *Time*, 4 September 1950.

the time of the kidnapping, had spent the best part of eighteen months on the island, hiding with the locals, speaking their language, disguising himself as Cretan townsman or shepherd, dedicating himself to intelligence-gathering, sabotage and the preparation of resistance. Attached, like Moss, to Britain's Special Operations Executive, a top-secret set-up tasked with causing trouble in enemy territory, he had already been rewarded with an OBE. The name of this young officer was Patrick Leigh Fermor.

The tale that follows this Introduction is Leigh Fermor's own account of the abduction of General Kreipe. It is published here, in its entirety, for the first time. When he wrote it, in 1966–7, Leigh Fermor was already on the path to great acclaim as a writer. *A Time of Gifts* and *Between the Woods and the Water,* the classic chronicles of his journeys as a young man traversing pre-war Europe, were still some years away, but in 1950 he had published *The Traveller's Tree,* an award-winning account of his recent travels in the Caribbean, and, three years after that, *A Time to Keep Silence,* an impression of monasteries and monastic life in England, France and Turkey. *Mani: Travels in the Southern Peloponnese* appeared in 1958 and *Roumeli: Travels in Northern Greece* in 1966. A novel, *The Violins of Saint-Jacques,* was published in 1953.

It may seem strange that a man of Leigh Fermor's experience and literary flair should not have written sooner about the kidnap. But he and Moss were friends and seem to have agreed early that the latter – who, unlike Leigh Fermor, had kept a diary of the operation – should tell the story first. Back in England in early 1945, Leigh Fermor had actually acted on Moss's behalf during an initial search for a publisher (a search that the War Office terminated on security grounds when it emerged that many of Moss's cast of British officers, mentioned by name in his text, were still engaged in behind-the-lines warfare).* It is certainly

---

* While corresponding with SOE about the manuscript, Leigh Fermor expressed uneasiness with aspects of Moss's portrayal of Crete and Cretans. 'It is not a very good book – too much is made of too little,' he cautioned, 'and there are too many clumsy literary references and insistence on a socially O.K. background

likely that Leigh Fermor had no desire to steal his friend's thunder; and it may be significant that he finally put pen to paper only after Moss's early death in 1965.

Leigh Fermor began writing his version at the request of Barrie Pitt, editor of *Purnell's History of the Second World War*, a mass-market anthology published in weekly editions in co-operation with London's Imperial War Museum. The idea behind the series, which was overseen by the military historian Basil Liddell Hart, was to produce rounded and respected studies of different aspects of the conflict that would add something significant to the historical record. Contributors ranged from modern historians to soldiers who had taken part. Articles were feature-length.

When giving Leigh Fermor the commission in the spring of 1966, Pitt had asked for 5,000 words deliverable by November. Not a man who always made editors' lives easy, Leigh Fermor penned over 30,000 and submitted them in instalments. The last of these reached Pitt nearly eleven months late. Pitt was pleased with neither the delay nor the length. Constrained by his own deadlines and a strict word limit, he brought on board a journalist to cut the text down to the requisite size. The reduced version that duly appeared in *Purnell's History of the Second World War* was, as a consequence, dramatically shorter: 25,000 words had gone. Much of the style and colour had been stripped away, too, replaced by a businesslike prose. In a brief editor's note, Pitt introduced Leigh Fermor as 'that most talented and charming of poets', commented that 'the Gilbert and Sullivan strain still runs strongly in the British ethos', and, quoting Kreipe, called it the story of the 'Hussar stunt' in

---

at home; and an attitude of patronage to the Cretans that hints that they were only fairly gentle savages . . . However, Hamish Hamilton [the prospective publisher at that moment] is going to make pretty drastic editorial revisions, so it may eventually emerge as what it should be: a young man's unpretentious account of an exciting adventure.' P. Leigh Fermor to Colonel D. Talbot-Rice, 9 April 1945, TNA HS 9/507/4. Moss had his own reservations, too, and did make subsequent revisions. But, as he explained in the preface when his book was eventually published, he was also convinced that his version ought to remain loyal to the perspective of the young man who wrote it.

Crete.* Leigh Fermor is said to have been unhappy with the changes. There was little he could have done to prevent them.

The restored manuscript, reproduced here, is important. Leigh Fermor had been asked to write an account of Kreipe's abduction. That was what was commissioned and, once the cutting was done, that was what was printed. But what he had produced – the original text – had been much more than that. As his biographer has written, the story he told in 'Abducting a General', the title he gave his piece, was 'not so much an adventure as a confession, a tribute, a plea for understanding . . . above all, a paean of praise to Crete and the Cretans'.† To explain that, it is necessary to acknowledge the strength of his connection to the Cretan people and place the kidnapping against the backdrop of his wider experiences on the island. It is essential, too, to recognise the link – direct or not – between the abduction of General Kreipe and the barbaric murder, months later, of hundreds of Cretan villagers at the hands of the German garrison.

In December 1933, aged eighteen, Patrick Leigh Fermor had left London to walk to Constantinople. It took him over a year to reach it. By then, the Continent had become more or less his home. During the next four years he spent only a scattering of months in England. Charismatic and well connected, he eked out his existence with some inherited money here, some translation work there, making friends easily, staying with them frequently, and travelling widely. In 1939, when news reached him that Britain had declared war on Nazi Germany, he was living in Romania. He returned directly to join up.

At first Leigh Fermor was accepted as a candidate for a commission in the Irish Guards. Sudden illness stalled the process, leading to a long and boring sojourn at the Guards Depot at Caterham. Then the Intelligence Corps stepped in. Impressed by

* P. Leigh Fermor, 'How to Steal a General', in Purnell's *History of the Second World War*, Vol. 5, No. 7 (c. 1969–70).
† A. Cooper, *Patrick Leigh Fermor: An Adventure* (London: John Murray, 2012), p. 340.

his languages – his pre-war wanderings had honed his French, German, Romanian and Greek – it offered a fresh path to a commission and the likelihood of a quicker route into action. With Axis pressure threatening to spread the war to South-east Europe, where he had so recently lived and travelled, Leigh Fermor shared the assessment that he might prove useful.

Officer training followed, then courses in military intelligence and interrogation, which he completed just in time to be dispatched to the Mediterranean as a member of the British Military Mission sent to help the Greeks, whose country the Italians, in October 1940, had invaded. Lieutenant Leigh Fermor was attached as a liaison officer to the Greek Third Army Corps. That contact did not last long. In April 1941, a savage German blitzkrieg swept through the Balkans, knocking Greece out of the war and driving the last British troops from mainland Europe. Remnants of the latter managed to scramble their way to Crete, the largest of Greece's islands, and bolster the British garrison there. Among them was Leigh Fermor.

Crete, too, was soon under attack, as the Germans, seeking to press their advantage, launched a major airborne assault. The fighting lasted days, the defenders included Cretan men, women and children, but the likely outcome was never much in doubt. Leigh Fermor, who had been attached as an intelligence officer to the British infantry brigade positioned around the capital, Heraklion, was one of the survivors whom the Royal Navy managed to evacuate to Egypt before Crete finally fell.

It was in Egypt that Leigh Fermor joined the Special Operations Executive, the unorthodox organisation whose task was to encourage resistance and carry out sabotage behind enemy lines. It is not difficult to see why he appealed as a recruit. Worldly, well travelled, confident and independent – 'Leigh Fermor does not submit willingly to discipline,' a staff officer would write of him stuffily, 'and I think requires firm handling' – he was just the type who seemed suited to SOE's irregular line of work.* His first

* 'Major Leigh Fermor DSO', Lieutenant Colonel E. G. Boxshall to SOE's

job was as an instructor at a training school in Palestine, teaching students bound for enemy territory how to handle weapons. Then, in the spring of 1942, fresh orders came through: he was to return to Crete to work clandestinely as an SOE agent.

By 1942, to be sure of holding the island against any Allied attempt to wrest it back, a strong Axis force was in occupation: tens of thousands of troops, rising to a peak of 75,000 in 1943, overlording a local population of just 400,000. Not without reason, the Germans came to call it *Festung Kreta*: Fortress Crete. In the mountains, a few guerrilla bands were active. So were a scattered handful of British officers sent in to lend support, gather intelligence, spread propaganda, harass the garrison and attempt, under the enemy's noses, to round up and evacuate Allied stragglers left stranded when Crete was captured. Landed, covertly, by a British-crewed Greek fishing boat, Leigh Fermor joined them in June 1942. He was to remain on the island for the next fifteen months.

During that period, the tide of war in the Mediterranean turned decisively in the Allies' favour. In North Africa, the victory at El Alamein and major landings in Morocco and Algeria were the catalyst for advances that, by the spring of 1943, had seen the Allies secure the Mediterranean's southern shores. That summer, Allied armies overran Sicily. In September, when a war-weary Italy surrendered, major landings in southern Italy saw the Allies return in force to mainland Europe for the first time in two and a half years. But in Crete not a great deal changed. The island remained firmly in the enemy's grip. The population stayed mostly compliant, hating the occupation but incapable of doing much to throw it off. Hopes of Allied landings ebbed and flowed but no liberation came.

On the rare occasions when British raiding parties went ashore to attack the island's airfields, terrible reprisals wreaked by German troops were graphic reminders of the risks of resisting. Two attacks by British special forces, the first in June 1942, the second in July

---

Security Section, 29 March 1945, TNA HS 9/1068/1.

1943, led the Germans, on both occasions, to execute fifty Cretan hostages in response. Many more were murdered in September 1943 after one guerrilla leader, Manoli Bandouvas, who had been encouraged by news of the Italian surrender to believe that the Allies might finally invade, decided suddenly to fight the Germans in the open. His men killed several before he saw his mistake and pulled back. German retaliation was swift and brutal. Seven villages south-east of Heraklion were burned to the ground and over five hundred Cretans, including women and children, shot. Generalmajor Friedrich-Wilhelm Müller, Kreipe's predecessor as commander of the 22nd Airlanding Infantry Division, was the officer who issued the orders. His actions earned him the nickname, 'The Butcher of Crete'.

SOE personnel at large on the island were well aware of the perils of working clandestinely. They also appreciated the extent to which their own presence and activities put the Cretans, too, in danger. The Germans knew that the British had men on Crete engaged in subversive warfare. From time to time, drives were launched into the mountains to catch them. Homes were burned. Local helpers and couriers were run to ground and killed. But though SOE, too, suffered casualties (among them Leigh Fermor's wireless operator, a young Greek from the Dodecanese, who, in late 1942, was captured, tortured and shot), most emerged unscathed. Their survival, they knew, was due in no small part to the selfless protection and assistance they received from the Cretan population. Inevitably, strong and lasting bonds of mutual respect and affection developed.

'For purposes of movement he adopted simple disguise, dying [sic] his hair, growing a beard and wearing Cretan dress,' reads a no-nonsense debriefing report of Leigh Fermor's experiences. Declassified only after his death in 2011, it provides a bracingly matter-of-fact glimpse of some of the risks he had run:

> He spoke to no-one except his trusted staff as his accent would have given him away at once. He had numerous false identity cards, and if stopped by the Germans he would have claimed to be a Cretan from the village named on the card.

Had he met a German patrol with an anti-British interpreter this cover would not have held . . . Had he been taken back to the village by a German patrol, there would have been no hope of his cover withstanding enquiry.*

Most British personnel faced such dangers. But as one SOE colleague remembered, Leigh Fermor had fitted Crete well. 'His pre-war experience of Greece combined with an instinctive phil-hellenism gave him an immediate grasp of local problems even though he had just arrived.'† His manner, too, was right. Warm, caring and courageous, a lover of language, dance and song, fascin-ated by other cultures, he forged life-long friendships with the Cretans, winning their trust and keeping it. 'He is still in Crete,' wrote the officer who recommended him for the Distinguished Service Order (he received an OBE) in April 1943, 'where his determination, devotion to duty and steadfastness of purpose have been invaluable in helping the local population to retain their faith in their allies. He is constantly hunted by the occupying troops.'‡

'On looking back,' Leigh Fermor wrote that month, 'my [first] six months seem to have been one long string of [wireless set] battery troubles, faulty [wireless] sets, difficulties about transport, rain, arrests, hide and seek with the Huns, lack of cash, flights at a moment's notice, false alarms, wicked treks over the mountains, laden like a mule, fright among one's collaborators, treachery, and friends getting shot.'§ The quotation comes from one of several reports for SOE headquarters in Cairo that Leigh Fermor penned

* Report by Captain Burr on debriefing of Major Leigh Fermor, c. December 1944, TNA HS 9/507/4.
† X. Fielding, *Hide and Seek: The Story of a Wartime Agent* (London: Secker & Warburg, 1954), p. 87.
‡ Recommendation for the award of the Distinguished Service Order, April 1943, TNA HS 9/507/4. Kreipe's kidnapping would earn Leigh Fermor an immediate DSO. Moss received the Military Cross.
§ 'Report No. 2' by Captain P. Leigh Fermor, 27 April 1943, Leigh Fermor Archive, National Library of Scotland.

while on the island. Most were drawn up in mountain hideouts, then couriered to the coast, to be sent out aboard small British boats and submarines that came quietly at night to drop off fresh men and supplies and embark evacuees. Original copies survive among Leigh Fermor's private papers. Providing hitherto hidden flashes of his characteristic writing style, they are markedly un-military in composition. A selection of extracts are reprinted here, after the text of 'Abducting a General', to underline the gruelling range of his experiences in Crete and the fact that they went far beyond kidnapping. They include his deeply personal account of what was undoubtedly one of the worst moments of his life: the tragic death of his guide and great friend, Yanni Tsangarakis, killed accidentally by Leigh Fermor's own hand.

Leigh Fermor's first mission to Crete ended in September 1943. He had started out in the western part of the island, working in the mountains where the principal guerrillas lurked. From February 1943 he had had charge of Heraklion, further east, where his role became more political: here, communists with complicated post-war ambitions were among the Cretans with whom he needed to deal. But it was not all politics. In the days after Italy's surrender, Leigh Fermor was able to help spirit to safety an Italian general before the Germans could get their hands on him. This was General Angelo Carta, the commanding officer of a division of 30,000 Italian soldiers. Leigh Fermor had not intended to leave the island with him. While assisting the Royal Navy with Carta's clandestine escape, however, he found himself stranded aboard a motor launch by a worsening sea and, as a result, was withdrawn to Egypt too.

It was back among his SOE compatriots in Cairo that Leigh Fermor tabled the plan for him to return to Crete with a hand-picked fellow officer – the choice fell eventually on Billy Moss – and kidnap a German general. Later, and, indeed, in the story he tells in these pages, he would trace his idea's inspiration to the autumn of 1943 and the successful evacuation, if not the abduction, of General Carta. In fact, the germ of a plan had been in place much earlier than that. Declassified SOE documents show that British officers had considered the wisdom and possibility of capturing a senior German officer as early as November 1942, when Xan Fielding, a close colleague of Leigh Fermor's in Crete, had had the idea of abducting General Alexander Andrae, *Festung Kreta*'s commander-in-chief. That plan was short-lived: Andrae was posted away. By the following summer, Fielding was thinking about seizing his successor, General Bruno Bräuer, while Tom Dunbabin, the senior SOE officer on the island, was wondering about kidnapping Generalmajor Müller in a coordinated operation. The latter, it was thought, might be especially vulnerable in or around his Cretan home: the Villa Ariadne. 'It should be easy to kidnap Muller,' Dunbabin wrote at the time. 'One of our agents is on good terms with his chauffeur, and he might be abducted on the road. Alternatively it sounds easy to break into the Villa Ariadne with a strength of about 20.'*

When Leigh Fermor drew up his plan, Generalmajor Müller was his intended target, too. By then, following the atrocities he had ordered in September 1943, 'The Butcher of Crete' was especially hated. Seizing him, so the reasoning went, was intended to deal a blow to German morale, while encouraging British missions on the island and the Cretan population to believe, at a time of fading hopes of liberation, that Crete's resistance remained effective. But the care that Leigh Fermor takes in 'Abducting a General' to explain the grounds for the planned kidnap, stressing, too, the steps taken to obviate the risk of enemy reprisals, is significant. By the time he came to write his account, he knew very well that the operation – which in the end saw Kreipe seized, not Müller – had been linked to a terrible event that occurred in Crete some weeks afterwards.

In August 1944, German troops swept through the Amari valley in the mountains of western Crete, burned a series of villages to the ground and killed over 450 people. '[C]omplete surprise was achieved,' recorded Tom Dunbabin, a helpless witness to the aftermath.

* 'Report No.1 (New Series)' by Lieutenant Colonel T. J. Dunbabin, covering period 8–23 September 1943, TNA HS 5/723.

The inhabitants of the raided villages were caught in their beds and a given number of hostages was taken in each village. These were selected either because of their relationship to some known person on the wanted list or because they looked sturdy fellows who would make good guerrillas. They were shot two by two and their bodies thrown into a building which was then blown up. One man escaped wounded from Kardaki to tell their story. The more attractive young women and a few men who were wanted by name were taken to Rethymno – the men succeeded in escaping en route. The remainder of the population were allowed to take one sheep or goat and as much as they could carry and were given two hours to get out. Much unnecessary suffering was caused – for instance one man of 73 had to carry his mother on his back for over three miles and pregnant women with a string of young children are [now] a common feature of the countryside. The enemy then began to plunder and loaded up everything in the village – sheep and cattle, food (the year's harvest had just been gathered in), furniture and clothes. As each house was gutted it was blown up or set on fire. This work is still going on and I can see the fires and hear the explosions as I write.*

Some inhabitants of the Amari, according to German communiqués, had invited that punishment for the assistance they were known to have given to General Kreipe's kidnappers four months before.

Dunbabin, who knew the Amari well, felt that the 'actual reasons' were more to do with a recent flare-up on the island of guerrilla fighting and British raiding, which had left dozens of German soldiers dead, coupled with a consequent German desire to retaliate and prevent further attacks, and the fact that the Amari valley had been known for years as a hotbed of support for the resistance.† Later, from Cretan

* 'Report No. 4 (Third Series)' by Lieutenant Colonel T. J. Dunbabin, covering period 20–30 August 1944, TNA HS 5/724.
† Ibid. Indeed, the Kreipe abduction was only one of several reasons put forward formally by the Germans to justify the reprisals of August 1944; others included the

friends, a distraught Leigh Fermor would hear similar explanations. Whether he ever accepted them is hard to know. 'These were consoling words,' he writes here; 'never a syllable of blame was uttered. I listened to them eagerly then, and set them down eagerly now.'

Considering the possible cost, it may also be wondered if Leigh Fermor was always convinced that the abduction was worth it. If he had doubts, he has not been alone. Concerns about the wisdom of kidnapping any German general were seemingly expressed at SOE headquarters even before Leigh Fermor's plan received the green light. Bickham Sweet-Escott, a senior and respected staff officer in Cairo at the time, would write in his own memoirs that he had considered the risk of German reprisals far too great to make an attempted abduction worthwhile, even with the hated Generalmajor Müller as the proposed target. 'I was asked whether I thought we should let this operation go ahead,' Sweet-Escott would recall.

> I made myself exceedingly unpopular by recommending as strongly as I could that we should not. I thought that if it succeeded, the only contribution to the war effort would be a fillip to Cretan morale, but that the price would certainly be heavy in Cretan lives. The sacrifice might possibly have been worthwhile in the black winter of 1941 when things were going badly. The results of carrying it out in 1944, when everyone knew that victory was merely a matter of months, would, I thought, hardly justify the cost.

'In spite of my pleadings,' Sweet-Escott went on, Leigh Fermor and Moss duly set off and ended up going for the 'comparatively harmless' Kreipe. 'I still have to be convinced that it was really worth the cost.'*

local murder of a German soldier, known British links to the valley, and the degree of local protection offered to various guerrilla bands. The long time lag between the kidnapping in May and the death and destruction meted out in August – uncommonly long by German standards – may also indicate that the abduction, while undoubtedly offering a convenient excuse, was not the principal precipitant of the Amari reprisals.
* B. Sweet-Escott, *Baker Street Irregular* (London: Methuen, 1965), pp. 197–8.

Today, the story of the kidnapping endures as a symbol of the spirit of Cretan resistance and as a tale of cloak-and-dagger buccaneering and wartime derring-do. At the time, British newspapers and radio broadcasts trumpeted details as propaganda. It remains difficult to attach much value to the operation otherwise. It had no strategic or tactical value: by 1944, when the Germans were expecting major Allied invasions at various points on the European mainland, Crete was a backwater. Abducting Kreipe may have embarrassed the island's German garrison and, by underlining the fact that a British-backed resistance existed on Crete and illustrating its capabilities, caused some to feel more vulnerable, but the blow to enemy spirits can be exaggerated.* Also, nothing useful in the way of intelligence was gleaned when the captive was eventually quizzed. 'Kreipe is rather unimportant,' reads a report by British interrogators after he landed in their lap. 'Anti-Nazi, possibly because events are trending that way. Rather weak character and ignorant.'† Certainly Kreipe was no monster, unlike Generalmajor Müller, who, taking command of Crete in July 1944, underscored

---

* With the invasion of Europe expected in the west and the tide of the war flowing firmly in the Allies' favour, German morale across the Mediterranean was already low by 1944. It also seems that Kreipe, once seized, may not have been especially missed, as one of his own officers, Ludwig Beutin, wrote to Billy Moss after reading his book. The soldiers were 'very surprised' that Kreipe had been kidnapped, Beutin recalled, but not particularly downcast: 'he was too little liked for that . . . It was much discussed in the officers' mess at that time, and many rakis were drunk to your health.' Beutin added, intriguingly, that one source of Kreipe's unpopularity was his impatience at roadblocks. 'He was very rude if his car was ever stopped as he considered the Divisional flags [displayed on his car] enough indication. People said – after the Abduction – that, shortly before, he had impatiently asked a soldier in Heraklion: "Don't you recognise your General's car?" After that, everyone took care not to examine it too closely . . .' Translation (1993) by Patrick Leigh Fermor of letter from Dr L. Beutin to W. S. Moss, 27 September 1950, Leigh Fermor Archive, National Library of Scotland. Long after the war, from 'a banker friend of mine in Hamburg' who had been on Kreipe's staff in Crete, Bickham Sweet-Escott would also hear the story of mess celebrations at the General's abduction (though in that version a German officer called for champagne). B. Sweet Escott, *Baker Street Irregular*, p. 198n.
† 'Additional Note by 2X', 23 May 1944, TNA WO 204/4208.

his murderous reputation by razing the Amari villages in August. At least one experienced officer at SOE headquarters – Jack Smith-Hughes, who had spent time as an agent in Crete and was running Cairo's Cretan desk when the kidnap took place – felt sure of a definite link between the kidnapping and the fate of those villages, noting that Müller had known the abduction had been meant for him.

Readers who compare Leigh Fermor's tale to *Ill Met By Moonlight* might find they identify more with young Billy Moss, who, fresh to Crete and clandestine warfare, finds himself suddenly ashore in a foreign land, dangerous, exciting and new. 'Abducting a General' is the perspective of a man of a different stamp. He knows the terrain. He speaks the language. He has networks of trusted contacts. While not careless of the risks, he is clearly accustomed to them: a few days before the kidnap, lunching in a Cretan house close to Knossos, Leigh Fermor, with moustache carefully bleached and hair darkened with burnt cork, cavorts happily with Cretan friends in the presence of three drunken German sergeants: 'attempts, bearishly mimicked by our guests, to teach them to dance a Cretan *pentozali*'. A host of Cretan guerrillas, guides and friends come and go in Leigh Fermor's text; all are testament to an emotional investment born of months of living among them, and to a belief that the full Cretan contribution to the Kreipe kidnapping – and to the war – demanded recognition and respect. This is the account of a sensitive man still bound to the island and its people.

Roderick Bailey
Oxford, June 2014

ABDUCTING A GENERAL

I

The sierras of occupied Crete, familiar from nearly two years of clandestine sojourn and hundreds of exacting marches, looked quite different through the aperture in the converted bomber's floor and the gaps in the clouds below: a chaos of snow-covered, aloof and enormous spikes glittering as white as a glacier in the February moonlight. There, suddenly, on a tiny plateau among the peaks, were the three signal fires twinkling. A few moments later they began expanding fast: freed at last from the noise inside the Liberator the parachute sailed gently down towards the heart of the triangle. Small figures were running in the firelight and in another few moments, snow muffled the impact of landing. There was a scrum of whiskery embracing, a score of Cretan voices, one English one. A perfect landing!

The Katharo plateau was too small for all four of the passengers to drop in a stick: each jump needed a fresh run-in. So, once safely down, I was to signal the all-clear with a torch. But the gap I had dripped through closed; our luck, for the moment, had run out. We took turns to signal towards the returning boom of the intermittently visible plane just the other side of the rushing clouds until the noise died away and we knew the plane had turned back to Brindisi. Our spirits sank. We were anxious lest the noise should have alerted the German garrison in Kritza; dawn, too, might overtake us on the way down.

Scattering the fires, whacking the loadless pack mules into action and hoping for a snowfall to muffle our tracks, we began the long downhill scramble. Tauntingly a bright moon lit us all the way. At last we plunged wearily through the ilex and the arbutus into the home-cave as the dawn of 6th February 1944 was breaking.

As it turned out, I stayed with Sandy Rendel★ in his cave for over a month. It was perched near a handy spring in the Lasithi mountains above the village of Tapais in Eastern Crete. Smoky, draughty and damp, but snug with strewn brushwood under the stalactites, it was typical of several lairs dotted about the island, each sheltering a signal sergeant, a small retinue of Cretan helpers and one each of a scattered handful of heavily disguised British Liaison Officers.

None of these BLOs were regulars. The only thing they had in common was at least a smattering of Ancient Greek from school. They all had a strong feeling for Greece and Crete and were deeply involved not only in the military grandeurs and miseries of the island, but, as the occupation lengthened, in every aspect of its life: the evacuation of our own stragglers, and (for training and re-entry) of resistance people on the run; in trying to help the bereaved, gathering information about the enemy, assisting commando raids and the dropping of arms and supplies, the organising of resistance and the composing of discord between leaders.

We became, as it were, part of the family. Our cave-sojourns were often brief. They were a cruel danger to the villages that supplied us with runners and with food and look-outs and we were often dislodged by enemy hunts in force. It was a game of hide-and-seek usually ending in a disorderly bunk to a new refuge in the next range. We could not have lasted a day without the islanders' passionate support: a sentiment which the terrible hardships of the occupation, the execution of the hostages, the razing and massacre of villages, only strengthened.

A time of bitter weather ensued: postponements, cancellations and false starts. Night after night Sandy and I set out with our

---

★ Captain (later Major) A. M. Rendel; later a distinguished member of the staff of *The Times*.

party for the plateau; again and again we heard the plane circling over the clouds; always in vain. Sergeant Dilley was permanently crouched over his set, tapping out, or receiving messages from SOE Headquarters in Cairo. (How far away it seemed!) We filled our long leisure lying round the fire, singing and story-telling with the Cretans, keeping the cold out with raki and wine. There were endless paper-games and talk and plenty of time, it soon turned out, to grow one of the moustaches that all Cretan mountaineers wear, and to get back the feel of mountain clothes: breeches, high black boots, a twisted mulberry silk sash with an ivory-hilted dagger in a long silver scabbard, black shirt, blue embroidered waistcoat and tight black-fringed turban; augmented, when on the move, with a white hooded cloak of home-spun goat's hair, a tall twisted stick, a bandolier and a slung gun, the apt epitome of a long and reckless tradition of mountain feud, guerrilla, and armed revolt against the Turks. There was time, above all, to think about the scheme on hand.

The idea of capturing the German commander had begun to take shape the autumn before. At the time of the Italian armistice, General Carta, commanding the Siena Division which occupied the easternmost of Crete's four provinces, hated and resented his Allies. It had not been hard, abetted by his counter-espionage chief, with whom I had long been in touch, to persuade him at a midnight meeting in his HQ at Neapolis to leave for Cairo with his ADC and several staff officers and the plans of the defence of Eastern Crete. His conspicuously pennanted car was sent north-east and abandoned as a false scent while we set off on foot south-west. (The Germans moved in next day.) There had been a hue and cry, searches, observation planes, dropped leaflets offering rewards; but we had got them through and embarked them in a timely MTB★ in a little creek near Soutsouro. We were in Mersa Matruh next afternoon and Cairo next morning. (I had been in the island nearly two years.)

★ [Motor Torpedo Boat.]

I put forward to the powers in SOE the suggestion of kidnapping General Müller. He commanded the 22nd Bremen ('Sebastopol') Panzergrenadier division based on Herakleion. It was the sort of action we all needed in Crete, I urged. The General was universally hated and feared – even more perhaps, than General Bräuer in Canea* – for the appalling harshness of his rule: the dragooning of the population in labour-gangs for the aerodromes, mass shooting of hostages, reprisal destruction of villages and their populations, the tortures and the executions of the Gestapo. The moral damage to the German forces in Crete would be great; a severe blow to their self-confidence and prestige. It would have its effect on us, too: our correct but uninspiring task – trying to restrain random action in preparation for the mass uprising we all hoped for – was an arduous, rather thankless one. Above all, it would have a tonic effect among the Cretans; our spirits, after reverses in the Viannos mountains at the time of the Italian armistice, were low; and one important guerrilla band – that of Manoli Bandouvas – was in temporary dissolution. The deed would be a triumph for the resistance movement which had kept the island so effectively and improbably united; and it would be a setback for the emissaries of the mainland left-wing movement who – fortunately too late – were trying to spread the same discord in Crete as that which was already tearing the mainland apart. The suggested action would be, above all, an Anglo-Cretan affair, a symbol and epitome of the bond which had been formed during the Battle [of Crete in 1941] and the thirty months which had followed. It could be done, I urged, with stealth and timing in such a way that both bloodshed, and thus reprisals, would be avoided. (I had only a vague idea how.) To my amazement, the idea was accepted.

There was no need to look for the first recruit. Manoli Paterakis from Koustoyérako in Selino in the far west had been my guide for over a year. A goat-herd and ex-gendarme, he had fought fiercely against the parachutists during the Battle. A year or two

---

* Both were executed as war criminals in 1946.

older than me, tireless, unshakeable as granite, wiry as a Red Indian, a crack shot and as fast over the mountains as the ibexes he often hunted, he was (still is) the finest type of Cretan mountaineer (there will be many such in this account). Completely unselfish, he was in the mountains purely from patriotism, and his mixture of sense, conviviality, stoicism, irony and humour, linked with his other qualities, made him more valuable than ten ordinary mortals. We had been companions on hundreds of marches and in many scrapes; had even, last summer, made an abortive joint attempt to sink a German tanker with limpets in Herakleion harbour. Neither of us had meant to leave Crete with the Italians – Manoli had been present at all the recent doings at Italian GHQ – but rough weather had hastened the vessel's departure, and, when we realised the anchor had been weighed, we were too far from shore to swim back in the dark. So, luckily, here he was in Cairo.

Finding another officer to take over during reconnaissances and to handle communications while I was away from our HQ – for lugging a wireless with batteries and a charging engine was out of the question – was harder; but luck still held. Bill Stanley-Moss, who had joined SOE from the Third Battalion of the Coldstream in the desert, was a worldly-wise and sophisticated twenty-two of great charm and looks; full of talents and high spirits and imagination, and a great friend and accomplice (with several other SOE companions – with whom we shared a house in Zamalek) in all the excesses which leave in Cairo excused or imposed. He jumped at the scheme and turned out to be an invaluable partner and perfect companion throughout.

Things began moving at once. I became a Major and a third pip descended on Billy's shoulder; I found George Tyrakis who, though younger, was of the same stamp as Manoli; he had been evacuated from his village of Fourfouras in the Amari for training a few months before, after long service, and attached himself to Billy. They got on at once, though at first they were mutually incommunicado except for grins and gestures. The rest of the party would be recruited in Crete. Preparations went forward with zest.

We planned to drop by parachute as near Herakleion as possible; Sandy Rendel, warned by wireless, found an ideal place for it. But, after training in Palestine and many delays, it was not till early January, after a tremendous Egyptian Christmas, that we flew to Tokra airfield near Bengazi. Here, with a score of people about to be dropped to Tito's partisans and the Greek mainland, we waited for days while the rain hammered on the tents; all in vain. Finally we were flown to Italy, arriving for the first night of *The Barber of Seville* in bomb-shattered Bari, now the swarming near-HQ of the Eighth Army. It was nice to be in a mainland European town again, but days of standing-by were hard to bear. But, at last, at half an hour's notice, we were being driven south at breakneck speed through the conical villages of Apulia. A converted bomber waited on the runway at Brindisi, and we took off in dismal February twilight.

Soon we were alone in the pitch dark except for the despatcher and the parachutes, four of them for us, the others for huge cylindrical containers. In these, and about our persons, were the gear for our operation: maps, pistols, bombs, commando daggers, coshes, knuckledusters, telescopic sights, silencers, a sheaf of Marlin sub-machine guns, ammunition, wire-cutters, sewn-in files for prison bars, magnetic escape devices, signal flares, disguises, gags, chloroform, rope-ladders, gold sovereigns, stealthy footwear, Bangalore torpedoes, every type of explosive from gelignite and gun-cotton to deceptive mule droppings which, they said, could blow a tank to smithereens; all the things indeed on which espionage writers dwell at such fond length; also Benzedrine, field dressings, morphine, knockout drops and suicide pills to bite under duress, if captured in the wrong clothes. I hoped we would use none of them, especially the last.

Much later on, shouting through the noise of the engine, the despatcher roused us from the torpor which is oddly usual at such times. There was moonlight all round and then the glittering crags of the White Mountains and Ida and a rush of cold wind from the hole the despatcher had opened in the floor. '*Spiti mas*,' Manoli said, looking down: '*Home.*' But it wasn't except for me.

★

The nightly circlings above the plateau were making the region too hot for us. The Kritza garrison was increased to a hundred – there were just under 50,000 enemy troops in the island – and the sweeps and ambushes, and occasional bursts of firing (although, in the dark, the Germans only managed to wound each other) were getting perilously near. Just as we were about to signal Cairo suggesting an alternative sea-borne rendezvous in the south, a message from them arrived proposing exactly this. (Billy and the others had left Italy for Cairo once more; finally they headed for Mersa Matruh.) Helped by a sudden thick mist, Sandy and I shifted out just in time, scattering with plans to join up later on.

March went by in travelling about in snowy and windy weather, gathering information, renewing contact and locating the where-abouts of old helpers that I would need. One item of news, late in March, came as a shock: General Müller was suddenly replaced by Kreipe, a General from the Russian front. All the delays seemed, retrospectively, more bitter. But, I consoled myself, the moral effect of the commander's capture would be just as great, whoever he might be. All I could learn was that he had commanded divisions on the Leningrad and Kuban sectors and was decorated with the Knight's Cross of the Iron Cross.

At last, at the beginning of April, Sandy, John Stanley – another old hand – and I, and a number of people for evacuation, were lying up in the mountainous prohibited zone above the south coast, not far from Soutsouro. We had a narrow shave a few miles inland, at the Monastery of the Holy Apostles: a heavily armed German foraging party arrived when we were in the middle of a feast. The Archimandrite Theophylaktos just had time to smuggle us into the cellar before they stamped in and insisted on a large meal. We crouched below listening to them among the Arabian Nights oil-jars until, heavily plied with wine by the Archimandrite, they reeled off singing.

2

At last, on the night of April 4th, the sound of a ship's engine answered our third night of torch signals; soon a sailor in a rubber dinghy was sculling into the cove and throwing a rope . . . In no time our evacuees were aboard, the ship vanished into the dark, and there, on the rocks, almost unbelievably after all our troubles, were Billy, Manoli and George. We loaded the stuff on the mules, said goodbye to Vasili Konios, our protector in the area, and headed inland for the long climb to comparative safety; settling at last in a high ravine full of oleanders, with the sea shining far below.

There was little sleep for the remainder of the night, or next day: too much to talk about. Raki and wine appeared, two sheep were slaughtered and roasted. Spring had suddenly burst over the island and the aromatic smell of herbs had hit the newcomers miles out in the Libyan sea. As I hoped, Billy was amazed by the spectacular ranges all round, and becomingly impressed by the dash, hospitality, kindness and humour of the Cretans.

Our unwieldy caravan could only move by night. We left at dusk, and a long trudge up and down deep ravines, halting now and then at a waterfall or a friendly sheepfold, brought us to Skoinia, where we lay up in Mihali's house. A day and a night were lost here, thanks to the visits of a string of our local leaders, including the huge Kapetan Athanasios Bourdzalis, who reappears later in these pages, and the arrival, in her mother's arms, of a little god-daughter of mine. All this gave rise to a banquet and songs, this time with well-placed sentries, from which we rose for an all-night march north-east across half the width of the island and over the dangerous edge of the Messara plain; circling round garrisoned villages, and using the device, in unoccupied ones, of barking '*Halt!*', '*Marsch!*' or '*Los!*' in the streets and raucously singing '*Bomber über England*', '*Lili Marlene*' or the '*Horstwessellied*', to spread ambiguity about the nature of our party.

At one point light rain filled the lowlands with flickering lights: hundreds of village women were out gathering snails brought out by the shower. Before dawn we reached the lofty village of Kastamonitza and the shelter of the family of Kimon Zographakis, who had been with us from the coast; a young man of great spirits and pluck and a former guide on commando raids. The generosity and warmth of all his family was doubly remarkable, as an elder brother had recently been captured and shot for his resistance work. We had to stay indoors by day, as there was a German hospital in the village: enemy voices and footsteps sounded below the windows. The upper chamber became a busy HQ of sorting maps and gear and sending and receiving runners; being hopelessly spoilt all the while by our hosts and their sons and daughters.

High in the mountains above Kastamonitza, in a cyclopean cave among crags and ilex woods overlooking the whole plain of Kastelli Pediada, lived Siphoyannis, an old goat-herd and a true friend: the very place for the party to hide for a few days while I went to Herakleion to spy out the land. I reinforced the party with two additions here, both old friends,* older than the rest, tough, robust, cheerful and unshakeable: Antoni Papaleonidas, originally from Asia Minor, who worked as a stevedore in Herakleion, and Grigori Chnarakis, a farmer from Thrapsano, just beneath us. The year before he had saved, in spectacular fashion, two British airmen who had baled out of a burning bomber.† The party – Billy,

---

* Both became god-brothers of mine later. Such a relationship – *synteknos* in Crete, *koumbares* in Greece – is important and binding. There are several in this story. One becomes a *synteknos* by baptising or by standing best man, to somebody's son or daughter.

† One of them, Flight Sergeant Jo Bradley, DFM, MM, before he was evacuated,

Manoli, George, Grigori and Antoni, with Kimon as liaison with the village (and, by runner, with me in Herakleion), and with Siphoyannis' vigilance up in those goat-rocks, near a good spring with a whole flock to eat – would be as secure as eagles. Everyone had taken to Billy at once, and he to them. He had abandoned his battledress with shoulder tapes for breeches and a black shirt and the cover name of Dimitri.

Meanwhile another runner – they usually carried their messages in their boots or their turbans – had brought Micky Akoumianakis hot foot from Herakleion. He was about my age, intelligent and well educated – none of the rest of the party were great penmen – and the head of our information network in Herakleion. By great luck, he lived next door to the Villa Ariadne at Knossos, just outside Herakleion; the large house, that is, built by Sir Arthur Evans for the excavation and restoration of the great Minoan site. Micky's father, now dead, had been Sir Arthur's overseer and henchman for many years. The villa was now the abode of General Kreipe.

My dress was readjusted by the family to look like a country-man's visiting the big city: bleached moustache and eyebrows were darkened with burnt cork. Dye sometimes runs, striping one's face like a zebra's. There are many Cretans fairer than me, but Germans looked at them askance and often asked for their papers, thinking they might be British, New Zealand or Australian stragglers disguised. My documents were made out to Mihali Phrangidakis, 27, cultivator, of Amari. We said goodbye and set off, boarding the ramshackle bus from Kastelli; there were a few country people taking vegetables and poultry to market in Herakleion. The conductor was a friend. But my Greek, though fast and adequate, was capable of terrible give-away blunders, so I feigned sleep. The only other vehicles were German trucks, cars and motorcycles. We were stopped at one of the many road-blocks approaching Herakleion and two Feldpolizei corporals asked for

---

became my signaller for several months, after my former signaller, Apostolos Evanghelou of Leros, had been captured and executed by the enemy.

our papers. About dusk, we were safe in Mihali's house in Knossos, peering out of the window with his sister.

The fence began a few yards away, and there, in its decorative jungle of trees and shrubs, with the German flag flying from the roof, stood the Villa. Formidable barbed wire surrounded it. (I had been inside it once, during the Battle, when it was an improvised hospital full of Allied – and German – wounded and dying.) We could see the striped barrier across the drive and the sentry boxes, where the steel-helmeted guard was being changed. Enemy traffic rumbled past, to Herakleion, three miles away. Due south rose the sharp crag of Mount Jouchtas; to west and south soared the tremendous snow-capped massif of Mount Ida, the birthplace of Zeus. North, beyond the dust of the city, lay the Aegean sea and the small island of Dia. East of the road, on the flank of a chalk-white valley dotted with vines, the bulbous blood-red pillars descended, the great staircase of the Palace and giant hewn ashlars, slotted for double-axes, of King Minos.

After his first astonishment at the project, Micky was alive with excitement. At discreet intervals we explored all possibilities of ingress to the Villa in case we were reduced to burgling it, seizing the General, and whisking him away. It might have been possible; Micky had known the inside of the house since childhood. But the triple barriers of wire, one of which was said to be electrified, the size of the guard and the frequency of patrols offered too many chances for mishap. Besides, to avoid all excuse or pretext for reprisals on the Cretans, I was determined the operation should be performed without bloodshed. The only thing was to waylay the General on the way home from his Divisional Headquarters at Ano Archanes, five miles away, and, to gain time, plant his beflagged car as a false scent.

Micky summoned Elias Athanassakis, a very bright and enterprising young student working in our town organisation, and we reconnoitred the route together. There was only one good place for an ambush: the point where the steeply banked minor road from Archanes joined the main road from the south to Herakleion at an angle which obliged cars to slow down nearly to walking pace. Clearly, owing to the heavy traffic on the main road, the deed would have to be done after dark – and very fast – on one of the evenings when, as Elias learnt, the General stayed late at the Officers' Mess in Archanes before driving home to dinner. This meant finding a hideout for us to lie up in near the road junction. Micky found it: the little vineyard cottage of Pavlo Zographistos outside Skalani, only twenty minutes' walk from Ambush Point – 'Point A'. When we asked him, he agreed at once to hide us.

The plan was beginning to take shape: Billy and I would stop the car, dressed up as Feldpolizei corporals. Sometimes, but seldom, there was a motorcycle escort: sometimes, other cars would accompany him. All this, assuming the ambush was a success, would land us with an unwieldy mob of prisoners, unless the attack could be launched or scrubbed in accordance with last-minute information. There was also the danger of stopping the wrong car. To avoid these hazards, Elias undertook to learn all the details by heart – silhouette, black-out slits, etc. – until the flags could clinch the matter at close quarters; and better still, he planned to lay a wire from a point outside Archanes to the bank overlooking Point A, along which an observer – himself – could signal with a buzzer the moment the General got into his car. A colleague on the bank would then flash the information to us by torch, and we, and the rest of the party who would be hiding on either side of the road, would go into action the instant the car appeared.

The risk from passing traffic still remained, possibly of trucks full of troops. Here we would have to trust to improvisation, luck, speed and darkness, and, if the worst happened, diversion by a party of guerrillas – un-lethal bursts of fire, flares all over the place, shoutings, mule carts and logs suddenly blocking the road to create confusion and cover our getaway with our prize. Still with reprisals in mind, we would only shoot to hurt as a last resort. It was vital for us to get into the mountains and among friends, away from the enemy-infested plain, and in the right direction for escape by sea, at high speed.

Micky and Elias were sorry to hear we couldn't evacuate our prisoners by air, in Skorzeny style: the Germans had put all the big mountain plateaux out of action for long-range aircraft by forcing labour-gangs to litter them with cairns of stones; and the smaller ones, even had they been suitable for small planes, were far beyond their fuel range from the airfields of Italy or the Middle East. But they cheered up when I told them that the BBC had promised to broadcast, and the RAF to scatter leaflets all over Crete announcing our departure with the General, the moment we were safe in the mountains. This would call off some of the heat, and confusing phenomena – flares, fires, unexplained musketry in the opposite direction to our flight, cut telephone wires, whispering campaigns and contradictory rumours planted within informers' earshot – could further perplex the hue and cry. Should our distance from communications delay action by the BBC and the RAF, it would be all-important, in order to exonerate the Cretan population, somehow to convince the enemy that their Commander's disappearance was due to capture, not assassination, and by a force under British command.

Many gaps and problems remained. Sending letters back to our base to cheer up Billy and the rest of the party, I spent the next days inside Herakleion with Micky and Elias and our other old helpers, shifting from one friendly house to another, exploring the streets and entrances and exits of the great walled town between twilight and curfew. Vaguely, as yet, an unorthodox method of getaway was beginning to form . . . Between whiles, there were secret meetings, not directly connected with the operation, with the group who ran the resistance and the information network in the city – doctors, dentists, lawyers, teachers, headmasters, reserve officers, artisans, functionaries and students of either sex, shop-keepers and the clergy, including the Metropolitan Eugenius himself – and visits to other cellars, reached through hidden doors and secret passages, where a devoted team reduplicated the BBC news★ for hand-to-hand distribution. After months in the mountains,

---

★ Ownership of an ordinary wireless set was punished by death.

there was something bracing about these descents into the lions' den: the swastika flags everywhere, German conversation in one's ears and the constant rubbing shoulders with enemy soldiers in the streets. The outside of Gestapo HQ, particularly, which had meant the doom of many friends, held a baleful fascination.

Back at Knossos, Micky and I were talking to some friends of his in a 'safe' house when three German sergeants lurched in, slightly tipsy from celebrating Easter. Wine was produced; Micky explained away the English cigarettes (brought in by Billy) which he had offered them by mistake, as black market loot from the battle in the Dodecanese. A deluge of wine covered up this contre-temps, followed by attempts, bearishly mimicked by our guests, to teach them to dance a Cretan *pentozali* in which we all joined.

Before rejoining the others in the mountains, we were standing with a shepherd and his flock having a last look at Point A when a large car came slowly round the corner. There were triangular flags on either mudguard, one tin one striped red, white and black, the other field grey, framed in nickel and embroidered with the Wehrmacht eagle in gold wire. Inside, next to the chauffeur, unmistakable from the gold on his hat, the red tabs with the gold oak leaves, the many decorations and the Knight's Cross of the Iron Cross round his neck on a riband – sat the General himself: a broad pale face with a jutting chin and blue eyes. I waved. Looking rather surprised at so unaccustomed a gesture from a wayside shepherd, the General gravely raised a gloved hand in acknowledgement and our eyes crossed. It was an odd moment, and, we thought as we watched the car disappearing, a good omen.

I got back to the hideout at last on April 16th, which was Orthodox Easter Sunday, the greatest feast of the Greek year. I had sent Billy warning before leaving (on foot this time) that our Herakleion agents had heard that the Germans suspected that a large body of parachutists had been dropped in the Lasithi mountains; a rumour due, no doubt, to the noise of the plane night after night; so it was best to keep a look out. But really it was all to the good: if they made a sweep, the enemy would find nothing; the Katharo was only twelve miles from our eyrie as the crow flies; but, in mountains like these, the distance could be multiplied many times; also, when our operation happened, there was a chance the enemy might think it was the work of this ghost commando.

Everyone was in high spirits; all the arrangements had worked perfectly. The party had been eccentrically increased by the arrival, escorted by a shepherd, of two Russian deserters who had been shanghaied into the German ancillary forces: a Ukrainian and a Caucasian, rather amusing scarecrows with whom Billy, whose mother was a White Russian, was able to converse. They could be incorporated into the guerrilla covering-and-diversionary force. For this, Bourdzalis's band, which was lying up only twenty-four hours' march away, was the obvious one. I sent Antoni – a great friend of the old giant and a fellow refugee from Asia Minor – to bring him and fifteen men as fast as possible. Their arrival would be the signal for our departure for the target area.

Meanwhile, there was a paschal lamb roasting whole and a demijohn of wine for us all to celebrate our reunion and Orthodox Easter with a feast and singing and dancing. Scores of hard-boiled eggs dyed red were clashed together like conkers with cries of 'Christ is risen!' and 'He is risen indeed.' Those left over were propped up in a row and shot down for pistol practice. When all of them were smashed, after every toast, pistol magazines were joyfully emptied into the air in honour of the Resurrection. Though all the canyons sent the echoes ricocheting into the distance, the noise was quite safe in this dizzy wilderness. Anyway, Cretans are always blazing away. Siphoyannis had brought several neighbouring shepherds, and the dancing, to our songs underlined with clapping, was nimble, fast and elaborate. I was sorry nobody had a lyra – the light three-stringed Cretan viol, or rather Rebeck, carved from beech and played on the knee with a semicircular bow – as George was an expert player.

Next day was given over to planning with Billy and Micky and Elias, who had both come with me for the purpose. (Apart from them, only Manoli and George, utterly discreet, had been told of our plan and sworn in; new initiates were only sworn in when it was necessary for each of us to know the parts we had to play. On each in turn the news had the same electric effect.) We decided that the General's car should not only be used as a false scent, but a getaway device as well; it should whisk the General and some of his captors from the scene at high speed. Where? It would be tempting to drive due south across the Messara plain and embark at Soutsouro, or some other combe on the south coast. This obvious scheme had several drawbacks. Firstly, it would be obvious to the Germans too; they knew we used those waters; and the way back to the main party for our only driver – Billy – after planting the car far enough away, would be too long and dangerous. Secondly, we would be fast on the move, and thus off the air to Cairo, for some time. Thirdly, should the enemy pick up our scent, those excellent roads could transport the large garrisons of the plain to the empty forbidden zone of low hills along the coast in a couple of hours; if necessary, they could fill the region with all the Germans in the Fortress of Crete. A cordon along the waterline and another inland could prevent any craft putting in, and, by intercepting our runners, cut us off from our distant wireless links with Cairo. Finally, with our backs to the sea in that region of sparse cover, they could run us to ground.

Far better to let the car, like a magic carpet, deposit us close to high mountains, with friendly shepherds for guides and caves and ravines to hide in till the first furore should die down. Runners could move fast and freely there; we could pick up our broken links with Cairo, and, via SOE, with the BBC, the RAF and the Navy, and arrange an evacuation further west. Above all, even with a slow-moving General on our hands, we could move more quickly than enemy troops. We would find a mule for him and, if the country grew too steep, put together a rough-and-ready palanquin; and there was always pick-a-back . . . A glance at the map at once indicated the vast bulk of Mount Ida, sprawling across a quarter of the island and climbing to over 8,000 feet; a familiar refuge to most of us, but, to the enemy, a daunting and perilous labyrinth haunted by guerrilla bands and outlaws. Not even a garrison of 50,000 men could completely cordon off that colossal massif; there would be gaps. A single road ran westwards along the north coast, to Retimo and Canea. South of this, the foothills climbed abruptly to the famous guerrilla village of Anoyeia, above which the welcoming chaos soared. North of the road and a couple of miles further west, a footpath ran four miles down the Heliana ravine to the sea. The point of junction would be the perfect place to leave the car. The place sprang to mind as, last year, I had waited three days there for Ralph Stockbridge and John Stanley to land by submarine. (They had announced their safe arrival by releasing carrier pigeons.) We could indicate to the enemy that we had left with the General by similar means, and scatter the path with corroborative detail.

There was only one drawback to this – Herakleion is girdled by a high Venetian city wall – unless it was an advantage: the only road from Point A to this desirable region ran clean through the heart of the city. It had one way in and one way out; there was a huge enemy garrison and numerous road-blocks and check-points; Anoyeia was twenty miles the wrong side of the city. There was no way round.* But, we reasoned, after dark in the blackout, the occupants of the car would be dim figures; all that the people in the street could see, and then sentries and the patrols and the parties at the check-posts, would be the hats and two figures in German uniform in the front; and a shout of '*Put that light out!*' would stop them from peering closer. Point A was only four miles from the town; with any luck we would be through it and away within half an hour of the capture; even less. The car would be

---

* There was a branch road, eight miles west of Herakleion, which turned left and ran through Tilisso to Anoyeia (and nowhere else), ending a mile short of the village. It was out of the question to take this; Anoyeia would have been hopelessly and glaringly compromised. Also, after the General and his escort had taken to the hills, the way back to the road fork and along the main road to the submarine path would be an extra twenty miles, too far for a non-driver (me). Something was sure to go wrong and wreck the whole scheme. Unfortunately I was the only one who knew the path to the submarine point; but I hoped I could get the car along a shorter distance without mishap.

observed driving normally in the streets, then leaving Herakleion westwards. Why not? By the time his staff began to grow uneasy, or the car was discovered – when, I hoped, the story of our submarine flight would come into play – we would have a long start up the side of Mount Ida.

Micky and Elias and I had discussed these possibilities in Herakleion; Billy's thoughts, from poring over the map, had been heading in a similar direction; Manoli and George, when they were called in, leaped at the idea. Now that the scheme was decided, it seemed the only possible one. The results of a mishap in the town were too disastrous to contemplate; but a plunge straight into the enemy stronghold with their captured commander would be the last idea to occur to them. We were excited and hilarious at the prospect and Micky and Elias sped back to Herakleion.

Next day our wait was relieved by watching two squadrons of RAF bombers attacking Kastelli aerodrome. There was a lot of flak, but several large blazes and columns of smoke indicated heavy damage. Each explosion evoked delirious cheers and all the planes headed back for Africa intact. Next morning, after marching a day and a night non-stop, Bourdzalis arrived with his men. They were festooned with bandoliers and bristling with daggers '*like lobsters*', as they say, but some of their arms were poor. (We could help here.) A few had been mustered in a hurry to complete the old giant's nucleus. The oldest were white haired and heavily whiskered, the youngest had scarcely begun shaving. They were all in the hills out of pure patriotism and free of politics, and bent on striking a blow, whatever it might be. They refused the idea of a day's rest. We had a meal under the leaves. Our own party, by slipping on battledress tops above their breeches and boots, and replacing their turbans with berets, assumed a semblance of uniform; each, beside his Cretan haversack, was slung with several Marlin guns. Billy and I made a similar change.

We waited for dusk to conceal our little column, now twenty-five strong, and moved off down the glen. I wanted to get them all to Skalani in a single giant stride, but it was too far over those rocks in the pitch dark. One or two of the elder guerrillas fell out, rather understandably. We just managed to reach Kharasso when the sky was growing pale; we hid all day in the lofts and cellars of two friendly houses, and set off again, wined and raven-fed, at nightfall; striking due west, over flatter and thus more dangerous country. We waded through streams noisy with frogs and passed through villages where the device of shouting in German again came to our help. Soon after midnight the guerrillas, the Russians and some of our party were safely hidden in a cave with a door containing an old wine-press. A little further down the dried-up river bed, Billy, Manoli, George and I were soon under Pavlo's roof, only five miles from Herakleion and less than a mile from Point A.

3

Stealth was vital so close to a large enemy concentration: not a move in the open during daylight. Although no other houses were near, the vineyards were overlooked by footpaths on all sides.

Micky and Elias brought the news that the General habitually sat next to the driver; he often returned after dark; other officers sometimes sat in the back; his car was not always alone. Elias had elaborated – or simplified – the alarm system: by keeping a look out from a height in Archanes, he could watch the General as he left his HQ, or the Mess, for his car; then jumping on his bike, he could pedal like mad to a point where his end of the wire was concealed and send the information by buzzer along a much shorter length of line; a great improvement.

Micky produced German uniforms for Billy and me; I can't remember where from – they were their summer field grey; he had got some campaign ribbons and badges, lance corporal's stripes and caps; all quite convincing enough for the short time they would be seen. He even had a traffic policeman's stick with a red and white tin disc. We tried them on with our own Colt automatics on the webbing belts with their *Gott Mit Uns* buckles and commando daggers as side-arms. I had just shaved off my moustache and Micky was photographing us when Pavlo gave the alarm: four Germans approaching the house. We dashed upstairs and waited, listening, with drawn pistols, as they lounged in and talked to Pavlo and his sister Anna. They were only on the scrounge for chickens and eggs; but when they had gone, we all had a stiff drink.

The best way of convincing the enemy that the operation was

an outside job under British command seemed to be to leave a letter prominently pinned up in the abandoned car. I accordingly wrote out the following, heading: To the German Authorities in Crete, April 23, 1944: –

Gentlemen,

Your Divisional Commander, General Kreipe, was captured a short time ago by a BRITISH Raiding Force under our command. By the time you read this both he and we will be on our way to Cairo.

We would like to point out most emphatically that this operation has been carried out without the help of CRETANS or CRETAN partisans and the only guides used were serving soldiers of HIS HELLENIC MAJESTY'S FORCES in the Middle East, who came with us.

Your General is an honourable prisoner of war and will be treated with all the consideration owing to his rank. Any reprisals against the local population will thus be wholly unwarranted and unjust.

> *Auf baldiges wiedersehen!*
> *P. M. Leigh Fermor*
> *Maj., O.C. Commando*
>
> *C. W. Stanley Moss*
> *Capt. 2/i.c.*

P.S. We are very sorry to have to leave this beautiful motor car behind.

We put wax seals from our rings after the names, for fun, and because such emblems were unlikely to be worn by partisans. It looked convincingly unlocal. I thought the message and the tone would be more convincing in English than in my German, which is fluent but as full of faults as an equally imperfect Greek German-speaker's might be. The important-looking envelope, fitted with

a safety pin, was addressed in the three languages in bold characters and tucked in the side pocket of my new outfit.

There were gaps that needed filling in the ambush party. Two
were filled at once, by Nikos Komis (like Grigori, from Thrapsano)
and Mitzo Tzatzas of Episkopi, both of them steady, quiet mountain men who had been our guides for the last two days. The
third, Stratis Saviolakis, was a uniformed policeman – invaluable
in itself – from Anapoli in Sphakia. (All proved admirable.) About
the fourth, Yanni, enrolled at the last moment as a guide for the
Anoyeia area, little was known, but he seemed all right. We slept
at last, hoping to act next day. Everything was ready.

But next day the General returned to Knossos early in the afternoon, so it was off for another twenty-four hours. Anticlimax
and slight deflation. Much worse, Stratis, returning from his *soi-
disant* policeman's rounds, told us that a few of the guerrillas,
suffering understandable claustrophobia in their wine-press, had
begun to stray into the open now and then; their presence had
become widely known. There was nowhere else to hide them;
so, alas, I would have to let them go; the risk was too great. I
had meant to brief them on the impending action, and their
dispositions and roles, at the last moment. Now, slinking to the
wine-press after dark, I told them that plans had been changed,
thanked them for all their help and willingness, and gave them
all our surplus Marlin guns. Bourdzalis and I exchanged hugs and
then set off at once. He was a fine old man.*

I was sorry to see them go; this sudden drop in manpower
reduced our scope; we were more dependent on good luck. But
our chances of going astray through over-elaboration were lessened
too; our party had gained in lightness and flexibility.

Micky told me he had run across Antoni Zoidakis in Herakleion.
This was splendid news. Antoni, who was from the Amari, the
other side of Mount Ida, had been involved in our work for years,
hiding and helping to evacuate stragglers and assisting us in a

---

* I never saw him again. He was killed in tragic circumstances later that year.

hundred ways. I sent word begging him to join us, and in the small hours here was that familiar figure sitting on my bed in his old policeman's jacket, his lean, shrewd and cheerful face lit up by an oil dip as we talked and smoked till dawn.

Pavlo and his sister were getting anxious about our presence in their house; not without reason. We all removed to the shelter of a clump of young plane trees in a deep dried-up river bed a little way off, where we had to lie without moving all day. German sweeps of the region were rumoured. Worse still, Pavlo brought me a letter from the local EAM leader,[*] mysteriously addressed to me by name – 'Mihali', that is. It held a strong hint that he knew what we were there for (perhaps it was a guess based on the closeness of the German HQ), followed by a threat of betraying us 'to the authorities', to remove the danger of our presence from the area. I sent back a quieting and ambiguous answer, hoping the guerrillas' departure would lend colour to the words; hoping, above all, that action that night would get us out of the area.

The odds against us were mounting up. Anxiety, though it left the old hands untouched, hung in the air. I was worried about Yanni the guide. It needed much outward cheerfulness and optimism to keep spirits from flagging. We passed the time talking and reading out loud. The afternoon wore on, and when Elias and Strati, who were watching the road, sent word that the General had not left the villa all day, things began to look black. The sun set after an interminable day of immobility; but now, at least, we could stand up and move about. I drew an outline of the car in the dust with a stick and we rehearsed the ambush by starlight until we all had our roles and our timing pat; then we lay about singing quietly till we fell asleep.

Anna, ever more anxious than before, brought us all a basket of food at daybreak, and more disquieting rumours. We had a growing feeling of isolation. Between the acting of a dreadful

[*] [Ethniko Apeleftherotiko Metopo (National Liberation Front); left-wing resistance movement.]

thing and the first motion, all the interim is like a phantasm or a hideous dream. The dream became more hideous still when Yanni the guide was smitten by a seizure, brought on, perhaps, by the tension of waiting: frothing lips, meaningless articulation, moaning and strange contortions followed by semi-catalepsy, prone among the myrtle bushes. We had to leave him there,* as rain drove us to a still remoter cache, and we never saw him again. Dodging singly in Indian file from cover to cover, we followed Pavlo uphill where we all huddled together in a damp and shallow cave, passing a bottle of *tzikoudia* from hand to hand. We were just in time; the sudden drizzle filled the landscape with snail gatherers. It was a bleak scene and the operation seemed to be receding further and further into improbability.

Yet, when word came from the road that the General had left for his HQ at the usual time, we suddenly realised that tonight was the night. Total calm descended on us all. It was as though everything, now, were out of our hands. *Le vin est tiré, il faut le boire*: we all knew what we had to do.

As soon as twilight blurred the scene, Billy and I changed into our German uniform, the others slung guns and we followed Pavlo and Strati downhill and across the vineyards, making loud German noises whenever we passed a shadowy homing vine-tender. It was dark when we reached Point A. We took up our positions in the ditches a yard or two north of the join in the roads. Billy and I settled on the east side, furthest away, then Manoli, Grigori and Antoni Papaleonidas; George, Antoni Zoidakis and Niko, in that order, on the west side. Further on, high on the bank, Mitzo was posted by the buzzer. Strati joined him. Once in place, we exchanged friendly whistles. Calm silence reigned. Out of sight, at the other end of the wire, we knew, Micky was waiting; and, at his vantage point at Archanes, Elias would be leaning nonchalantly on his bike. It was 8 p.m.

During the hour and a half of our vigil a few German cars and trucks drove past at intervals, and a motor bicycle and side car,

* He recovered and came to no harm.

26

very close to us, all coming from the south and heading for Herakleion, nothing from the minor Archanes side road. Nice and quiet; but time seemed to pass with exasperating slowness. It was getting late; had there been a mistake somewhere? . . . Anxiety began to set in. On the tick of 9.30, Mitzo's torch flashed clearly three times. '*General's car*,' the signal meant. '*Unescorted. Action.*' Manoli gave me a squeeze on the elbow.

4

The two corporals stood in the middle of the road facing the junction, Billy right and I left. In a few moments a car was slowly turning the corner with stiff coloured pennants on both mudguards. Billy waved his disc and I moved my red torch to and fro and shouted '*Halt!*' The car came to a stand-still and we stepped right and left out of the beams of the headlights, which, in spite of being partly blacked out, were very bright, and walked slowly, each to his appointed door. The two flags were there; but perhaps only the driver was inside . . .

Through the open window I could discern the gold braid and the Knight's Cross and a white face between. I saluted and said '*Papier, bitte schön.*' The General, with an officer-to-man smile, reached for his breast pocket, and I opened the door with a jerk (this was the cue for the rest of the party to break cover) and the inside of the car was flooded with light. I then shouted, '*Hände hoch!*' and with one hand thrust my automatic against the General's chest – there was a gasp of surprise – flinging the other round his body, and pulling him out of the car. I felt a vigorous blow from his fist and a moment later he was lashing out in the arms of Manoli, and, as there were no passengers, of Antoni P. and Grigori as well. After a brief struggle, and a storm of protest and imprecation in German, the General was securely bound, Manoli's manacles were on his wrists and he was being hoisted bodily into the back. Manoli and George leapt in on either side; and Strati followed them. The doors were slammed shut and gun barrels were sticking out of the windows. I picked up the General's hat, which had come off in the struggle, jumped into the General's empty seat, slammed the door and put his hat on.

Billy was already calmly at the wheel, door shut and engine running. Half a second after I had opened the right-hand door, Billy had wrenched open the left. The driver, alarmed at the sudden chaos, reached for the Luger on his belt. Billy struck him hard over the head with a life preserver, George pulled him out of the car and Billy jumped in, glanced at the petrol gauge, checked the handbrake and found the engine still turned on. George and Antoni Z. carried the driver, temporarily knocked out and bleeding, to the cover of the ditch. (When the two Antonis, Grigori and Niko set off with him – we were to meet on Mount Ida in two days – he was able to walk, but groggily.) Micky and Mitzo had rushed from their stations and suddenly, except for Elias, the whole party was there, leaning into the car or already inside it. Micky was craning through a window, shaking his fist and passionately shouting, '*Long live freedom! Long live Greece! Long live England!*' and, menacingly, at the General, '*Down with Germany!*' I begged him to stop, moved by our captive's look of alarm; there was already a daunting commando dagger at his throat.

A delirious excess of cheers, hugs, slaps on the back, shouts and laughter held us all in its grip for a few seconds. I suddenly noticed the inside light was still on: our very odd group was lit up like a magic lantern; so, as there was no visible switch, I hit it with my pistol-butt; reassuring darkness hid us once more. Billy released the brake and we drove off, exchanging farewells with the two parties remaining on foot. (When the others had left, Micky and Elias would hide their gear, clear up any give-away clues, dust over all signs of strife, then head for Herakleion, and, when the news broke, set helpful rumours flying.) All these doings, which need time to record, had only taken, from the time we signalled to the car, seventy seconds. Everyone had been perfect.

Less than a minute later, from the opposite direction, a convoy was bearing down on us; two trucks full of soldiers sitting with their rifles between their knees, some in steel helmets, some in field caps, rumbled past. Our voices sank to a sober whisper; we had only been just in time. (Where were they heading for, I wondered later. I hoped it was to smoke out that phantom raiding force in the Lasithi mountains.) The General was still dazed. '*Where is my hat?*' he kept asking; I had to tell him where. In a few minutes we were driving through Knossos and as we approached the Villa Ariadne, the two sentries presented arms, a third, warned by a fourth, raised the striped barrier. They must have been surprised when we drove on; the sentries stamped back to the stand-at-ease. I knelt on the seat, leant over the back and said the words I had been rehearsing as slowly and earnestly as I could: '*Herr General, I am a British Major. Beside me is a British Captain. The men beside you are Greek patriots. They are good men. I am in command of this unit and you are an honourable prisoner of war. We are taking you away from Crete to Egypt. For you the war is over. I am sorry we had to be so rough. Do everything I say and all will be well.*'

This little speech had a strong effect. '*Sind sie wirklich ein Britischer Major?*' '*Ja, wirklich, Herr General. Sie haben gar nichts zü fürchten.*' He again bewailed the loss of his hat and I promised to return it. '*Danke, danke, Herr Major.*' He was still shaken, but improving.

At this point Billy said: '*Check point ahead.*' I sat down again. Two men – as it might have been us – were waving a red torch in the middle of the road, there was a cry of '*Halt!*' Billy slowed down slightly. When they saw the flags the two men jumped aside, stood to attention and saluted. I returned it, and Billy accelerated again, murmuring, '*This is marvellous.*' '*Herr Major,*' came the voice from behind, '*where are you taking me?*' '*To Cairo.*' '*No, but now?*' '*To Herakleion.*' There was a pause, then, several keys higher in complete incredulity, '*TO HERAKLEION?*' '*Yes. You must understand that we must keep you out of sight. We will make you as comfortable as we can later on.*'

By this time houses were becoming denser beside the road and pedestrians and animals frequent, and the glow of booths, taverns and cafés; and soon another red light, a narrowing of the road and a cry of '*Halt!*' then another. We passed them in the same style as the first, and those that followed. At Fortetza, there was a forbidding wooden barrier as well. Again, the flags sent it sailing respectfully into the air. Soon we were inside the great Venetian city wall; the main street swallowed us up. The Marlin guns, lowered now, were held ready behind the doors.

The General had sunk below window level in a vice-like grip. George's dagger was still threateningly aimed and when German voices grew loud beside the car, hands were clamped over his mouth. We were held up by a number of manoeuvring and reversing trucks, and soon by a cheerful swarm of soldiers pouring out of the garrison cinema. (It was Saturday night.) Billy calmly and methodically hooted his way through this mob; a swerving cyclist nearly fell off avoiding us. Creeping along, collecting many salutes as the soldiers cleared out of the way, we reached the turn by the Morosini fountain and headed left for the Canea Gate. It was the only way out of the town.

If anything went wrong on the way through, the plan was to drive fast for the Canea Gate, and, if the barrier there was down, charge it and break through, and then, if pursued, fire long bursts out of the back window and the sides and hurl the Mills grenades with short fuses which weighted down all our pockets. (We had plenty of spare magazines for our sub-machine guns and automatics.) Outside the Gate, we stood a chance of getting away. This powerful brand-new Opel must have been the fastest car in the island and Billy was a skilful and imaginative driver. With a long start we could make for the mountains at full speed, get out well before troops from Retimo, warned by telephone, could head us off from the west, send the car spinning down a precipice, and, after concealing the tracks, strike uphill. But, should there be determination *en masse* to stop us at the Canea Gate we would slew round fast and into the lanes – I had a good idea where, thanks to those wanderings with Micky after dark – leave the General tied and blindfold ('*Remember, General, we have spared your life! No reprisals!*'), block the way with the car and make a dash for it. There was a maze of alleyways, walls one could jump, drainpipes to climb, skylights, flat roofs leading from one to another, cellars and drains and culverts – as Manoli and I had discovered during our raid on the harbour – of which the Germans knew nothing. If cornered, we had plenty of grenades and spare ammunition and iron rations. Perhaps, by lying up, and with a bit of luck, there would have been a chance. The town was dotted with friends' houses and, after all, except for a handful of spies and traitors, the whole city would be on our side.

There was a clear run down the narrow main street to the Canea Gate. But as we approached the great barbican, which the Germans had tightened into a bottleneck with cement anti-tank blocks, there were not only the normal sentries and guards, but a large number of other soldiers in the gateway as well. The one wielding the red torch failed to budge; it looked as though they were going to stop us. Tension in the car rose several degrees. Billy slowed down – we had arranged for this eventuality – cocked his automatic and put it in his lap; mine was already handy; behind, we heard the bolts on the three Marlin guns click back. When we were nearly on top of them and one of the guard was approaching, I put down the window and shouted, '*Generals Wagen!*'

The words '*Generals Wagen!*' passed peremptorily from mouth to mouth; the torch was lowered just in time. Billy stepped on the accelerator, the soldiers fell back and saluted, the sentries jumped to the present. All this was acknowledged with a gruff goodnight and we drove through. We sailed through the check points (the other inmates of the car counted twenty-two from start to finish) with great smoothness. We passed John Pendlebury's grave on the left of the road. At last the check points and the long ragged straggle of suburb, were all behind us and we were roaring up the road to Retimo with the headlights striking nothing but rocks and olive groves. Mount Ida soared on our left and sea, just discernible, shone peacefully below.

A mood of riotous jubilation broke out in the car; once more we were all talking, laughing, gesticulating and finally singing at the tops of our voices, and offering each other cigarettes, including the General. They made him as comfortable as they could. I handed his hat back and asked him if he would give his parole not to attempt to escape; to my relief he gave it. I then formally introduced Billy. He had no German and the General no English, so civilities were exchanged in French, not very expert on either side. I then presented Manoli, George and Strati by their Christian names and for a moment the four figures behind all seemed to be formally bowing to each other. A bit later the General leant forward and said, '*Sagen Sie einmal, Herr Major, was für ein Zweck hat dieses Husarenstück?*' ('*Tell me, Major, what is the object of this hussar-stunt?*') A very awkward question. (We were passing the solitary *khan* of Yeni Gave, near our first destination; only twenty miles from Herakleion, but, thanks to the bad road, it was already past 11 p.m.) I told the General I would explain it all tomorrow.

We now had no local guide since Yanni's eclipse but Strati had served in the area as a young policeman and Manoli and I knew it a bit. We drew up at the bottom of a goat-track which, after a few hours' climb, would end at Anoyeia. We all got out and Manoli unlocked the handcuffs. The General was perturbed when he saw that I was going on with George. ('*You are going to leave me alone with these . . . people?*') I told him the Hauptmann would be in command and that he was under Manoli's special care. This sounded ambiguous, but there was something in Manoli's bearing that inspired trust. The party were to lie up outside Anoyeia and wait for us; Manoli and Strati knew who to contact for food and runners, for messages to our nearest wireless stations. I saluted, the General did the same (I was keen on setting this single note of punctilio in our rather bohemian unit). Billy and the General set off uphill, Strati leading, Manoli in the rear with his gun in the crook of his arm.

There was a certain amount of laughter from the slope when at last, after several stalls, the car wobbled off down the road in bottom; I just managed to get the thing along the two miles which led to the beginning of the track that ran down past the hamlet of Heliana to the submarine bay and the tiny island of Peristeri. We left the car conspicuously well out in the road. The floor had been purposely covered with fag-ends of Player's cigarettes; these clues were reinforced by a usurped Raiding Forces beret ('Who Dares, Wins') and an Agatha Christie paperback. We kicked up the pathway, running down it to plant a round Player's tin, and, further on, a Cadbury's milk chocolate wrapper. (If only we had had a sailor's cap . . .) The letter to the German authorities was prominently pinned to the front seat. Then – we couldn't resist it – we each broke off one of the flags which had served us so well. I gave mine to George who waved them both, saying, '*Captured standards!*' and shoved them in his sakouli* with the steel rods sticking out.

There was no path. It was only five or six miles to Anoyeia for a crow, but three times as far for us; all ravines, cliffs, boulders, undergrowth and thorns. Luckily there was a new moon. The only people we saw all night were two boys with pine torches hunting for eels in a brook. Hailed from afar they put us on the right track. Every hour or so we lay down for a smoke. The night was full of crickets and frogs and nightingales. The snow on Mount Ida glimmered in the sky, and neither of us could quite believe, in this peaceful and empty region, that the night's doings had really happened. The approach of dawn was announced by the tinkling goat bells of a score of folds waking up in the surrounding foothills and just above us we could see the white houses of Anoyeia spreading like a fortress along a tall blade of rock.

* [Colourful, woven rucksack.]

5

Anoyeia, the largest village in Crete, was too remote and isolated for a permanent garrison. High on the northern slope of Mount Ida, it is the key foothold for crossing the great range. Famous for its independent spirit, its idiosyncrasy of dress and accent, and its tremendous local pride, it had always been a sure hideout.

The year before, Ralph Stockbridge and I had baptised the daughter of a brave and dashing man and local leader, Stephanogiannes Dramountanes. Our god-brother had been killed – shot down while trying to make a break for it by jumping over a wall with his hands tied after a German encirclement of the village – but I knew we could find all the backing we needed from other god-relations and friends, and to spare.

There was no hint of it as we climbed those windy and dawn-lit cobbles. I was still wearing German uniform. For the first time I realised how an isolated German soldier in a Cretan mountain village was treated. All talk and laughter died at the washing troughs, women turned their backs and thumped their laundry with noisy vehemence; cloaked shepherds, in answer to greeting, gazed past us in silence; then stood and watched us out of sight. An old crone spat on the ground. The white-whiskered and bristling elders with jutting beards shorn under the chin were all seated outside the coffee shop; baggy-trousered, high-booted, headkerchiefed men leaning on their gnarled sticks. (I knew a few of them but the German Waffenrock★ and the missing moustache were an impenetrable disguise.) They stopped talking for a moment,

★ [Uniform.]

then loudly resumed, pointedly shifting their stools to offer their backs or their elbows in postures of studied hostility. Doors and windows slammed along the lane. In a moment we could hear women's voices wailing into the hills: *'The black cattle have strayed into the wheat!'* and *'Our in-laws have come!'* – island-wide warnings of enemy arrival. We were glad to plunge into a side alley and the friendly shelter of Father Manoli's house. But Father Chairetis, one of the celebrants of the baptism and a great friend, was out. The kind old priestess, retreating down the corridor in alarm, refused to recognise me; it is amazing what a strange uniform and the removal of a moustache (or of the beards that we all grew at one time or another) would do. *'It's me, Pappadia, Mihali!'* *'What Mihali? I don't know any Mihali.'* Deadlock.

Alerted by a neighbour, the priest arrived, and at last, amid amazement and then laughter, all was well. The village were told we were harmless scroungers; later, that we had left. The give-away garments were peeled off. My god-brother George Dramountanes was soon there, and other friends and helpers arrived discreetly. A runner was found in a moment who would carry our news to Sandy – nearly a hundred miles away to the south-east now, in the mountains above Males and Ierapetra, and another for Tom Dunbabin, of whom more later, the other side of Mount Ida. Raki and meze appeared under the great arch of the house and sitting on the cross-beam of her loom plucking a chicken in a cloud of feathers the priestess was all smiles and teasing now. (Nobody had heard of the capture yet. What was happening at Knossos, Archanes, Herakleion? Had the car with the letter been discovered? How were the others getting on?)

Thank heavens for Strati's police uniform. He soon appeared. The ascent had been laborious – the General's leg had received a bang during the struggle at the car – but safe. They were now sheltering in a gulley a mile or two away. He and Manoli had found two eager and nimble shepherd boys from a nearby fold; enjoined to speed and secrecy by their fathers they sped south and east with messages from Billy to the same destination as mine; two strings to each bow. (It was a wise measure against the stormy days that we foresaw.) A basket of food and drink was stealthily dispatched and I was to join them after dark with a guide and a mule for the General.

In the late afternoon the noise of an aircraft flying low over the roofs brought us all to our feet. Running up the ladder to the flat roof, we saw a single-winged Fieseler Storch reconnaissance plane circling above the roofs moulting a steady snowfall of leaflets. It wheeled round several times, then whirred its way up and down the foothills, and vanished westwards still trailing its white cloud, then turned back towards Herakleion. Several leaflets landed on the roof. We took them downstairs. '*To all Cretans*', the text went in smudged type still damp from the press.

> *Last night the German General Kreipe was abducted by bandits. He is now being concealed in the Cretan mountains and his whereabouts cannot be unknown to the inhabitants. If the General is not returned within three days all rebel villages in the Herakleion district will be razed to the ground and the severest reprisals exacted on the civilian population.*

The room was convulsed by incredulity, then excitement and finally by an excess of triumphant hilarity. We could hear running feet in the streets, and shouts and laughter. '*Just think, they've stolen their General!*' '*The horn-wearers won't dare to look us in the eyes!*' '*They came here for wool and we'll send them away shorn!*' How had it happened? Where? Who had done it?

The priest, who was in the know, and god-brother George, Strati and I lowered our eyes innocently. I told them it was the work of an Anglo-Cretan commando; mostly Cretan; '*And you'll see! Those three days will go by and there won't be any villages burnt or even shooting!*' (I hoped this was true. I seemed to be the only one in the room undisturbed by the German threat and I prayed that urgency would lend wings to the messengers' heels and scatter our counter leaflets and the BBC news of the General's departure from the island. Had the Germans found the car yet, and followed our paper chase of clues down to the submarine beach?)

37

'*Eh!*' one old man said, '*They'll burn them all down one day. And what then? My house was burnt down four times by the Turks; let the Germans burn it down for a fifth! And they killed scores of my family, scores of them, my child. Yet here I am! We're at war, and war has all these things. You can't have a wedding feast without meat. Fill up the glasses, Pappadia.*'

An hour after sunset, our two parties now rejoined, we were winding up a steep and scarcely discernible goat path. On a mule in the centre, muffled against the cold, in Strati's green gendarme's greatcoat, with Manoli by his side, rode the General, or rather, Theophilos: the words '*Kreipe*' or '*Strategos*' had been forbidden even as far back as Kastamonitza. Billy told me they had had a German alarm during the day and had moved their hideout: Could it have been George and me? They'd even managed to get some sleep. The General, they all said, had been reasonable and co-operative; his most immediate worry, which he repeated to me during our first rest for a smoke among the rocks, was the loss of his Knight's Cross. I said it had probably come off in the struggle; perhaps it had been picked up during the clean-up, in which case I would see it was returned, and he thanked me. Apropos of the leaflets, which I translated, he said: '*Well, you surely didn't expect my colleague Braüer to remain inactive when he learnt of – my rape?*' (*Mein Raub*).

'*No, but the Germans won't catch us.*' (I touched a handy ilex trunk here.) '*The Cretans are all on our side, you know.*' '*Yes, I see they are. And, of course, you've always got me.*' '*Yes, General, we've always got you.*' At another of these halts, he said, after a sigh and almost to himself, '*Post coitum triste.*' I was astonished at this comment, and had told him that only a few minutes before, and far out of earshot, Billy and I had decided that this phrase exactly suited the brief mood of deflation that had followed the capture. '*It's all right for you, Major,*' the General said, '*military glory, I suppose. But my whole career has come to bits. (Meine ganze Karriere ist kaput gegangen.) The war is over for me, as you said. To think that my promotion from Generalmajor to Generalleutnant has just come through!*' His heavy face – he had a massive jutting chin, grey straight hair cropped at the sides but long enough to fall over his forehead, and blue eyes – looked morose and sad. '*I wish I'd never come to this accursed island.*' He laughed mirthlessly. '*It was supposed to be a nice change after the Russian front . . .*'

We both laughed. It was all rather extraordinary. He was a thickset, massively built man, but not fat. He was wearing, unfortunately for the journey ahead, the same lightweight field grey as we were, with the loose ski trousers of mountain troops, and, thank heavens, thick mountain boots. There were many ribbons over the left breast pocket, the Wehrmacht eagle over the right, the Iron Cross First Class – won at the battle of Verdun, low on the breast, but no shield on the left arm with the map of the Crimea like the rest of the Sebastopol division he had commanded till a few hours ago. The red tabs and the gold oak leaves blazed with newness. No eye-glass, no Mensur* scars. He was the thirteenth son of a Lutheran pastor in Hanover and professional soldier to the backbone. He must have had, in surroundings where there was more scope for it, a solid and commanding presence.

In the small hours, we climbed off the track and curled up on the bracken floor of an old shepherd's hut; the fire in the middle lit up a conical stone igloo, cobwebbed and sooty and lined with tiers of cheeses like minor millstones and dripping bags of whey. George and I, except for an hour interrupted by comings and goings on the divan running round the priest's living room, hadn't slept since Skalani.

We all rose again in the dark and continued our journey. As dawn broke, we were hailed from an over-hanging ledge: it was one of Mihali Xylouris's lookouts, sitting with a gun across his knees. In a moment he was bounding down the hill, he threw his gun aside with a yell and flung his arms round me, Billy, Manoli, and George, only stopping just in time at the astounded General. It was one of my honorary god-brothers, Kosta Kephaloyannis, about nineteen, as lithe and wild looking, with

* [Duelling.]

39

bronze complexion, huge green eyes and flashing teeth, as a young panther.

Other lookouts had joined us from their spurs and soon we were in Xylouris's cave, surrounded by welcoming guerrillas. Mihali was the Kapetan, or leader of the Anoyeians, in succession to Stephanoyannis, and all the Anoyeian names – Dramountanes, Kephaloyannis, Chairetis, Sbokos, Skoulas, Manouras, Bredzos, Kallergi and many others – were represented there, and all armed to the teeth. Mihali, with his clear eyes, snowy hair and moustache and white goatskin cape, was one of the best and most reliable leaders in Crete. There were formal introductions, and the cat, as far as the General's whereabouts and the identity of his captors went, was out of the bag.

Here, too taking refuge under Mihali's wing, were a cheerful trio of English colleagues. John Houseman, a young subaltern in the Bays, John Lewis, heavily booted and bearded, and, miraculously, Tom Dunbabin's wireless operator and his set. Informed, like all the other stations in the island, via Cairo, of our messages I'd sent to Sandy, Tom had sent his wireless station on to Mount Ida to help us. As though by a miracle, our communications problem was suddenly solved. I joyfully wrote out a signal, breaking the news, urging the BBC and RAF action and asking for a boat in any cove the Navy found convenient south of Mount Ida. Fortunately a time schedule to Cairo was just coming up; we could wait here, arrange things at our ease, cross Ida, slip down to the sea, and away. With any luck the BBC announcement and the RAF leaflets would have convinced the enemy that we'd left and reduce their opposition to a token show of force or even none at all.

It was a day of meetings: four figures were spotted through binoculars coming from the east: the two Anthonys, Grigor and Niko; but no driver. I was filled with misgiving. We all – the reconstituted abduction party that is – went aside among the boulders. '*It was no good, Kyrie Mihali*,' Antoni Zoidakis explained, handing me a German paybook and some faded family snaps. He was very upset. Alfred, the driver, had been still half stunned, poor devil. He could only walk at the rate of a tortoise. They'd almost carried him across the plain to the eastern foothills; then, during the afternoon, the hunt was up: motorised infantry had detrucked in all the villages round the eastern flanks of the mountains and begun to advance in open order up the hillside. There was nothing for it: if they left the driver behind for the Germans to overtake, the whole plan, and the fiction of non-local participation, was exploded; the entire region would be laid waste with flame and massacre; if they stayed with him, they themselves would have been captured. There was only one thing for it; the enemy were too close to risk a gun's report: how then? Antoni leant forward urgently, put one hand on the branching ivory hilt of his silver scabbarded dagger and, with the side of the other hand, made a violent slash through the air. '*By surprise. In one second.*' '*He didn't know a thing,*' one of the others said. There was a deep crevasse handy and lots of stones; he would never be found. '*It was a pity, he seemed quite a nice chap, even if he was a German.*'

It was shattering news; the silence of malefactors hung over us, broken at last by Manoli. '*Don't fret about it! We did our best. Just remember what those horn-wearers have done to Crete, Greece, Europe, England!*' Predictably, he repeated the proverb about the wedding feast. We all stood up. I told them they'd acted in the only possible way and it was true.

After an hour trying to get the coded message away, the operator discovered that some vital part of the set had gone dud; a part, moreover, irreplaceable in Crete; it was a lack only to be remedied by sea – like our own problem – or by parachute. Both these, of course, could only be arranged by wireless contact. The circle was hopeless.

At this point, our first runner to Tom arrived back with the news that nobody in the south knew where he was; he'd sent us his wireless, and vanished into thin air – up with a bad attack of malaria. There were two other stations in the province of Retimo far away in the north-west; but Tom was our only link with them. Anyway in the present commotion, they would almost certainly

be on the move. The messenger also brought news of troop movements at Timbaki, Melabes, Spyli and Armenoi: columns of dust
were heading towards Mount Ida, from the heavily garrisoned
Bad Lands of the Messara; observation planes were scattering
leaflets over the southern foothills. A runner from Anoyeia brought
reports of identical enemy doings in the north: lorried infantry
disgorging in all the foothills as far west as the great monastery
of Arkadi (a notorious haunt of all of ours, until it was blown),
where the German troops had bombarded the Pro-Abbot Dionysios
and his monks with the same question that they were asking
everywhere: Where is General Kreipe? But so far, and most untrue
to form, there had been little violence, few arrests, no shooting.
There was a glimmer of hope.

Otherwise, the scene was beginning to cloud. Mihali Xylouris
and god-brother George picked out an escort for the next stage
of our journey; our god-brother would accompany us. '*Whatever
happens*,' Mihali said, '*we'll block the way for the Germans. We know
all the passes. We can blow them to bits; and if they get on to your
tracks, we'll shoot into the gristle!*' – i.e. to kill. I begged him not to
fire a single shot, just to keep cover, watch where the enemy was
and let us know if they got anywhere near. (The Germans nearly
always stuck to the main paths; when they wandered away from
them, they usually got lost; all guides commandeered locally would
lead them to the foot of unscaleable cliffs and over landslides and
up and down steep torrent beds of shank-smashing boulders.)
Everything ahead was a looming wilderness of peaks and canyons,
and in the rougher bits it would be impossible for a large party
to keep formation, or even contact, except at a slow crawl which
could be heard and seen for miles by the mountain's denizens;
there would be plenty of warning. The whole massif was riddled
with clefts and grottoes to hide in. We must all vanish into thin
air and let the enemy draw a total blank. I explained why and
asked Mihali to speak the commando rumour and keep mum about
us (a tall order). The General remounted and we left after fond
and grateful farewells. The Andartes and the three Anglo-Cretans

waved their crooks and their guns in valediction till the track hoisted us out of sight.

For the General, breaking bread with Mihali and his men and us must have seemed rather odd: the many signs of the cross before falling to and then the glasses clashed together with the usual resistance toasts: '*Victory!*', '*Freedom!*', '*Blessed Virgin stand close to us!*', '*May she scour the rust from our guns!*' and '*May we die without shame.*'

Mihali and his band were scrupulously polite; but they found it hard to wrench their glance from our strange prize. The shaggiest and most unlettered Cretan mountaineers often possess a charm and grace of manner, even if the supper is only goat's milk and rock-hard, twice-baked shepherd's bread, amounting to a very high style, which, after the handful of petit-bourgeois collaborators in Herakleion which can have been his only social experience of Greeks, must have come as a surprise to the General.

It was thought wiser tonight to do without a fire. Drinking a lot of raki to keep warm, we sang for a while: the old Cretan insurrectionary song '*When will skies clear?*', elaborate rhyming couplets, a *rizitika* – a foothill song – '*My swift little swallow*', '*An Eagle was Sitting*' in the minor mode, and '*Philedem*' – a song with a Turkish tune that I was so fond of that it had become a nickname.

Through lack of covering, Billy, the General and I ended up, not for the last time, by all three sleeping in the wireless cave under the blanket, with Manoli and George on either side, nursing their Marlin guns and taking it in turns to sleep. Verminous as such places always were, it was a greater torment to my bedfellows than to me, already coarsened by nearly two years of onslaught.

A curious moment, dawn, streaming in the cave's mouth, which framed the white crease of Mount Ida. We were all three lying smoking in silence, when the General, half to himself, slowly said:

43

Vides ut alta stet nive candidum Soracte

– the opening line and a bit of one of the few odes of Horace I know by heart. I was in luck.

> '*Nec jam sustineant onus*,' I went on,
> '*silvae laborantes geluque*
> *Flumina constiterint acuto*'

and continued through the other stanzas to the end of the ode. After a few seconds silence, the General said: '*Ach so, Herr Major.*' For five minutes the war had evaporated without a trace.

A few hours' climb brought us within hail of Kapetan Petrakoyeorgi's outposts, high on the shoulders of Ida. We were soon in the toils of a welcome even more triumphant and demonstrative than Mihali's. Petrakoyeorgi – tall booted, bandoliered, robust, warm-hearted, voluble and, with his sparkling eyes and twirling moustache and beard, full of charm – was one of the three original guerrilla captains of the Occupation; taking to the hills at the invasion, they had all suffered many hardships. The other two were Captain Satan of Krussona: he was evacuated early on, with the Abbot of Preveli, to Cairo because of ill health, where, alas, he died. The other was Manoli Bandouvas at present in Cairo too, where we had evacuated him after his disastrous attack on the Germans in the Viannos mountains. He returned later and remustered a large force.

Heavy and buffalo-moustached Petrakoyeorgi was brave and ruthless, a sort of Tamerlane; I always liked him in spite of his glaring faults, of which the most glaring was a headstrong instability of temperament which made him prone to rash acts: doings which in a moment could bring down in smithereens a year's careful preparation by the rest of the resistance movement. I think the General was rather impressed by his grand air and hospitable and expansive manner: also, perhaps, by the large quantity of the arms of the men who swarmed the rocks in large numbers, with many familiar and friendly faces among them; the gun-running trips and parachute drops were beginning to bear fruit.

Petrakoyeorgi gave us a new guide and Antoni Z, who came from the Amari, on Ida's southern flank, left in advance with two more to send back as runners to a rendezvous the other side of the watershed. We'd worked out a system of bonfires to indicate the route if he could find any cunning way between the German concentrations. All said that large numbers were gathering round the southern slopes. If no way existed for the moment, he would send us word to go to ground and stay put.

6

We were hardly out of earshot of the Andartes' goodbyes before troubles began. The steepness and irregularity of the track were too much for the mule; back it had to go and the General, to his despair and ours, had to continue on foot up a slippery and collapsing staircase of loose boulders and shale and scree. We took it in turns to help and he did his best; the pace grew slower, the halts more frequent; soon we were far above the ilex belt. The last stunted mountain cedar vanished, leaving us in a stricken world where nothing grew and a freezing wind threatened to blow us off our feet. Then deep snow turned every step into torment. As we crossed the steep watershed between the plateaux of Nidha and Zomithos and the ultimate summit of Holy Cross, over 8,000 feet high, mist surrounded us and rain began to fall.

We stumbled on, bent almost double against the blast; no breath or energy was left even for objurgation: still less for anyone to say that not far off was the Ideon cave which had sheltered the childhood of Zeus. (From the summit, on a clear spring or autumn day, the whole island, from the westernmost peaks of the White Mountains to the eastern massif of Sitea, lies extended like a chart. To the south the Libyan sea rises like a curtain which is bare except for the Paximadia islands and Gavdos with its satellite islet, where the wind called Euroclydon nearly wrecked St Paul; to the north-west hover the Taygetus mountains of the Peloponnese, to the north-east Santorini and the outer Cyclades; due east, a sprink-ling of the Dodecanese, the faraway peaks of Rhodes, and bold travellers have climbed the Taurus range in Asia Minor.) Now, in the approaching dusk, all was rain and wind, and obliterating cloud. We couldn't even take advantage of the last of the daylight without the first of Antoni's go-ahead beacons on the first ridge to the south. We huddled with chattering teeth in the ruined shards of a hut.

The rain stopped and the sky grew clearer. We spotted the first fire, a faint star of light far down the mountainside. As we made our way down the hill through the darkness it was soon masked by an intervening spur. At least the snow furnished a pale glimmer underfoot. When it stopped, all was dark. Masking our torches, we were crawling and sliding down avalanches of stone. When this came to an end, we were swallowed up in the tree belt which surrounds the bald summit like a tonsure: ragged cedars at first topiaried by the wind nearly flush with the rocks; then a thick tangle of ilex and mountain holly and thorns.

The mountain steepened to the tilt of a ladder. It was channelled and slippery with rain and each footfall unloosed a landslide of shifting stones. We were descending, hand over hand, through what seemed, in the dark and the wind, to be a jungle of hindering branches, spiked leaves, and vindictive twigs. It was appalling going for everyone; for the General, in spite of our help, it must have been an excruciation. There was not a glimmer of Antoni's guiding fires in the dark void below. One of Petrakoyeorgi's men said he knew of a sheepfold on a hidden ledge. We divined its whereabouts in the small hours by the sudden tinkle of a flock awakened by our crashing. After wolfing down some of the shepherd's bread and cheese, we all fell asleep by his fire; then, before daybreak, staggered on like sleepwalkers to a cave mouth and crawled through the bushes into a subterranean grotto to hide there till next nightfall.

It was a measureless natural cavern that warrened and forked deep into the rocks, and then dropped, storey after storey, to lightless and nearly airless stalactitic dungeons littered with the horned skeletons of beasts which had fallen there and starved to death in past centuries: a dismal den, floored with millennia of goats' pellets, dank as a tomb, cobwebbed and gleaming, in the twilight to which the overhang reduced the cloudy day above, with snails' tracks and damp; but thanks to the ilexes that masked the entrance we could light fires of wet wood which were just worth the aching eyes and the choking smoke under which we slept or moved about like ghosts. The day before we had been reduced to hunting for wild herbs. Today the water the shepherd had given us was soon finished. Cretan mountaineers are as expert in finding a spring or a trickle in the most unpromising landscapes as doctors at locating a pulse: but each one in turn came back with a pitcher still empty.

A photograph★ from Billy's records of this journey shows the General, hardly discernible in the penumbra, lying reading. Under Stratis' green gendarme's greatcoat with its white corporal's stripes on the cuff I could just see the General's field grey tunic with its General's red tabs. These were now augmented by my khaki battle-dress blouse with parachute wings over the breast (eagerly unstitched from the right arm and re-sewn there the day after dropping) which I had put round his shoulders. (I had wriggled back into my thin German tunic.) It struck me that things were really getting confused. I must have laughed for the General asked me why. I pointed to our outfits and said, '*I was only thinking that they'd have to shoot both of us now.*' The General responded to this bad taste joke with one of his wintry smiles and shifted closer to the flames. It was the only flicker of levity in a day of great stress.

Several of us had, at one time or another, lived in scores of caves on Mount Ida, shifting from one to another as rumour pinpointed our whereabouts or enemy searches made it wiser to change lodgings: strange winter sojourns cowering away from the monsoon-like downpours outside or falls of snow whose only advantage was the ease of tracking and catching hares: caverns, sometimes, whose windings magnified the thunder of autumn storms to such volume that the mountain seemed to be splitting all round us. There were nights of talk and song, or of listening,

---

★ In the picture, he is reading a book; by a process of elimination, I think it must have been either *Les Fleurs du Mal* or *The Anabasis*, the only non-English books we had.

while some hoary shepherd incapable of signing his name, intoned by heart as many of the epic ten thousand lines of the *Erotocritos* as he could fit in between sunset and dawn . . . For the Cretans, veneration and gratitude halo the mountain. It is the island's crown and the impartial sanctuary of everyone in flight from justice or injustice and its mythological aura is deepened by the Himalayan remoteness and by the awe that hovers over Mount Sinai on Cretan icons. All my sojourns have been strange; none, though, as strange as these, huddling with the General and a volume of Baudelaire or Xenophon between us in the mountain's heart, while below us in a ring his army prowled like the troops of Midian. Antoni's hastily scribbled note when it arrived and his runner confirmed the gloomy rumours we had heard on the way up. Troops were assembled in force in all the villages and preparing next day to link up in what sounded like a human daisy chain to intercept all descent from the mountain and then advance uphill in a general comb out. '*In God's name come tonight,*' Antoni urged in his letter. It sounded as if the operation were due tomorrow morning. A mule for the General would be waiting at a certain meeting place.

As soon as it was dark enough, we emerged and clambered down through the dripping woods. Soon, on a tufted ledge, a friendly figure was waiting with a fine beast; its howdah of a saddle was padded with coloured blankets. We were heading roughly in the direction of Nithavris, the highest Amari village on the southern slope of Ida. As soon as we had joined Antoni, we were to slip between Nithavris and Apodoulou or between Nithavris and Kouroutes – all staunch landmarks but now, presumably, full of the enemy – and head across the Amari valley and hide some-where near Antoni's own little village of Ay Yanni and Aya Paraskevi. We reached the tryst – a trough for flocks made out of a tree trunk scooped hollow in a clump of holm oaks – early; but there was no Antoni; George and Manoli ranged the hillsides with soft whistles and calls, but drew blank. We waited two hours with growing misgivings. Had he run into trouble? There was nothing for it but to push on down.

Gradually the slopes grew milder; there were fewer loose stones under foot. The moon and the stars were hidden by cloud and not a light showed in the pitch dark. But, by an occasional dog barking, the bray of a donkey, an untimely cockcrow or a random voice on the hillside we could feel the presence of villages. We were able to move with more silence and circumspection now. (When setting out, Manoli had muffled the bell which was slung round the mule's neck on a string of blue beads to ward against the Evil Eye.) Rain came swishing down: *'Marvellous for the olives,'* Manoli murmured. We waded through a stream and began to climb again. The rain turned to sleet. At last the village of Aya Paraskevi was only half an hour away. The Germans would have sentries out, perhaps patrols; better to stop there. We piled into a ditch mercifully overgrown with cistus, thyme and myrtle; protection from view, but not from the rain.

Antoni's failure to arrive was an enigma full of anxiety. In his letter, which Manoli and I had read in the cavern, his injunctions had been so urgent and precise. With our heads hooded in a jacket we read it through again, out loud, by shaded torchlight: *'In God's name come tonight!'* Wait! There was something else after the *'name'* – the fold in the paper came here; friction, rain or sweat, soaking through the runner's turban, had all but obliterated two letters: *hu!*; that is, *'Don't.'* I translated it to Billy. All of us, except the General, gazed at each other in amazement and conjecture in which, despite the water which was beginning to rise above our ankles, a very faint hope began to glimmer.

Next morning, George went to the village to find out what was happening. Two hours later we could see him strolling unconcernedly back with Antoni, who was carrying a big basket. When they reached us they jumped into the ditch and Antoni said with a wide grin: *'What are you doing here, boys? You ought all to be dead!'* He had been unable to believe George at first when he had told him that we had arrived. *'How did you get through? The whole place was full of them. Hundreds, especially where you came down. You must have walked clean through the middle.'* He made the sign of the cross several times. *'God exists! You ought all to build churches. What, churches? Cathedrals!*' The real rendezvous had been for that night. Where were the Germans now? '*All gone up Mount Ida, after you and the General.*' A shepherd who had made a bolt for it downhill a couple of hours before had said that a party of fifty of them had crashed past his hiding place, shouting – here Antoni dropped his voice to be out of our prisoner's earshot – '*Ge-ne-ral Krei-pe, Ge-ne-ral Krei-pe,*' at the top of their voices! '*But you could have been quite all right in that cave. As it is, you are lucky to be here, my children.*'

Gregori said, '*What have you got in that basket?*' Antoni unpacked bread, cheese, onions, a dish of fried potatoes, some lamb and a napkin full of *kalitsounia!* – crescent-shaped fritters full of soft white cheese and chopped mint. Then a big bottle of mulberry raki came out and a handful of little tumblers. '*This will warm you up,*' he said filling them: '*White flannel vests all round.*' He splashed politely over to our guest with the first one, saying, '*Stratege mou* ['My General'],' then to the rest of us. They went down our throats like wonderful liquid flame. '*And here,*' he said pulling out a gallon of dark amber wine, '*red overcoats for all.*'

Local feeling in Crete is passionate and competitive. Many villages are as justly proud of their fame as were the ancient city states, and in questions of distinction during the resistance there is a human and excusable tendency among the inhabitants of some of them to claim a monopoly of courage and sacrifice. So it is rather a surprise that not even the haughtiest of them would dream of denying the special position of the Amari: perhaps they are disarmed by the fact that the Amari is a whole galaxy of villages, not an isolated rival; it is a position, moreover, which the Amari, out of modesty and distrust of rhetoric – or is it because there is no need? – would never dream of revindicating. A union of geography, the events of the war, and the temper of the inhabitants singled out the Amari for its especial role. It is the only eparchy* in the island with no coast, a deep wide valley running north–west

* An eparchy is a county, the administrative subdivision of a nome, or province.

to south-east airily slung like a hammock high above sea level between the south side of Mount Ida and the north side of Mount Kedros: a magnificent spreading crag, worthy satellite to Psiloriti, whose southern slopes drop nearly sheer, and to tremendous depths, into the Libyan sea. The little farmstead of Sata, in the south-east, overlooks the whole of the Messara plain, the aerodrome of Timbaki, inland from its tremendous bay and all the bad lands down to the Kophino mountains on the far south, at the other end of which, at Soutsouro, the party had landed so long ago. Yerakari, on the southern flank of the pass at the north-western end of the Amari, is the highest village in Crete. The valley is only about twenty miles long, and at its widest under ten miles broad. It seems much more, a huge and complex Highland glen with cherry orchards on its flanks and springs gushing down the mountainside, olive groves, a few vineyards, even some pale green patches of wheat sprinkled with poppies, shady ravines and tufted with walnuts, fig trees, plane trees and mulberries. There are old Turkish bridges and derelict water mills and, along the stream beds at the bottom, a flutter of poplars. A succession of beautiful white-walled villages is strung along the sides of the valley from end to end. To all of us, after months in the wild mountain tops, it seemed like Canaan.

Ever since the Battle the Amari had been a hideout from the enemy; hundreds of British and Commonwealth stragglers left behind at Sphakia or broken out of POW cages had been clothed and sheltered and fed here; it was a sort of transit camp on the way to secret evacuation at a dozen points on the rocky southern coast; guerrilla bands, harried from their native ranges, came here to lick their wounds; the place was a general haven and there was hardly a goat fold or ledge of rock or cave or olive grove or orchard on the mountainside that had not been the hideout of a BLO* with his signaller, W/T, guards and runners. All this was due to the spirit of the villagers and the harmony and the trust that prevailed between them.

* [British Liaison Officer.]

The place was notorious to the enemy; countless searches had been unable to find anything or to deter the Amariots. It is not so much the Cretan guerrilla tradition that flourishes here: there is all the courage, high spirits, hospitality, charm, humour and kindness, which, throughout the Cretan mountains, accompany their fiercer traits; the thoughtful literary, rather poetical strain which, in proverbs, marks the home of Retimo seems to hover almost palpably in the air here. They were just as determined to win the war as anyone in the mountains with a gun, and their losses, by the end, were terrible; but the particular task of the region, as vital and as difficult as attack, was one of preservation, rescue and sanctuary.

There were some immediate reasons for restrained rejoicing. All round us were the tried bulwarks of the Amari; we had leapt the enormous hurdle of Mount Ida; and the Germans were hunting for us in the wrong direction. Talking the matter over, some of us felt that the Germans had got on to our scent on Mount Ida; I didn't think this. As far as Antoni could make out, there had only been about a thousand troops in the Amari villages; and these figures are always doubtful and usually exaggerated. We had heard of considerable concentrations on the other slopes of the mountain – five thousand for the whole of Mount Ida, at the very outside. But there were also reports of serious searches north of the Herakleion–Retimo coast road – could they be prompted by our letter? – and in the Kophino mountains. We soon learned, too, that a strong force had thrashed through the Lasithi and Vianno. There were, in fact, chaotic troop movements everywhere and searches through all the most likely mountains within range of the General's capture. But specific information would have meant a far stronger local concentration.

Some rumours said that the Germans feared a general uprising planned, perhaps, to coincide with an invasion of the island. General Bräuer, in command of the West of *Festung Kreta* at Canea, had strengthened the guard round his HQ and moved nowhere without escort. We heard that the BBC had announced the capture of the General, but with their passion for the truth, and most unfortunately for us, they had said he '*was leaving the island*', instead of using the past tense; hence the island-wide search. No RAF leaflets so far. But all this meant, at least, that one of our runners must have got through to Sandy and we would be hearing from him soon. (If only Tom's wireless had been working! If only we could find him and, through him, the other stations in the north-west!)

We were now an appalling distance from our only link with Cairo. But there was one piece of marvellous news: six days had passed since the dropping of the leaflets threatening reprisals within three days; and, in spite of all the enemy activity and questioning and threats, no villages had been attacked and no hostages taken; nobody shot. This, again, pointed to our letter being taken seriously. (Perhaps, too, this unwanted clemency, after so unambiguous a threat, was prompted by the fear among the enemy of counter-reprisals on their vanished Commander.) Colour was added to this hypothesis next day. We had just moved to a better shelter in a clump of blackberry bushes, when an aeroplane flew down the valley and away towards the Messara – with black crosses on the wings, alas, not RAF roundels – shedding some leaflets. It had now been ascertained, we read, that the kidnapping was the work of '*hired tools of the treacherous British and the Bolsheviks. Those responsible would be mercilessly hunted down and destroyed.*' By implication, this very tame communiqué lifted the blame from the Cretans in general. Our relief was enormous. We had been living in dread.

The reaction to the capture all over Crete was, it seems, one of unbridled hilarity and jubilation. Antoni related all the rumours and talk of the villages: what a smack in the face for General Müller and the whole German garrison. And – a wonderful example of a Cretocentric theory of the universe among the simpler of the islanders – how furious Hitler must be. (None of the party had thought as far afield as this; presumably the remote event *had* been mentioned in the morning's reports; could there have been a brief outburst in the Wolf's Hole?) It was the same in Canea and Retimo and – we learnt from Micky and Elias who suddenly arrived, after walking from the bus halt at Retimo and wisely heading for Antoni's village – in Herakleion too; nothing but grins and innuendos in the street; almost overt rejoicing in fact; and, a little surprisingly, intrigued amusement, here and there, among the lower ranks of the Germans themselves; utter fury and bewilderment higher up. Micky, after the General had been introduced to the missing two of his captors, told him, through me, that all the guards of the villa were under arrest and his ADC was in prison, on suspicion of complicity. The General's blue eyes opened wide with disbelief, then he laughed delightedly. He couldn't bear him, the General told us. The man was a complete dunce.

These tidings were music to us, but everything else was very bad indeed. The immediate threat from the enemy was momentarily less than it had been. The nearest Germans were a long-established platoon at Krya Vryssi, three miles away to the south-west, round the shoulder of Mount Kedros. But everything else was in a disturbed and fluid state and full of conflicting movements and rumours. The garrisons of the Messara and Retimo could close the Amari at a moment's notice; and we would get warning: there were always the mountains and the caves; but our little circle in the blackberry clump seemed very vulnerable. (There were reasons for not seeking a recondite lair.)

Our biggest trouble was the breakdown of Tom's wireless set on Mount Ida. Had it been working, all our problems would have been solved. On top of this, the failure to contact Tom himself was perplexing in the extreme; he was the only Open Sesame to the other two stations. (What had happened, it later emerged, was this: having nobly sacrificed his set to us for fixing up the evacuation, he had been stricken down with malaria and had just managed, alone except for one companion, to creep to the north-west of the Amari and wrestle with it there in a remote cave. Then, as he was incapable of moving, he had so covered his tracks as to be, even to the innermost circle of Amari initiates, beyond finding. There were no means of his learning about the breakdown and thus no knowledge of our whereabouts or of our need to make contact with him.)

In all my signals to Cairo sent by runner to Sandy I had asked them, apart from announcing the news via the RAF and the BBC, to get the Naval section to send a boat near Saktouria on the night of May 2nd and, shore-signals failing, on the four following nights; to send us the two letters of the Morse alphabet we were to flash with our torches when we should hear the engines in the dark; and to signal all this information to all stations in Crete. This programme allowed us six days to cross Mount Ida and reach the appointed rendezvous on the first night. We had arrived in perfect time, for Saktouria – and this is why we were hiding in our present lair – was only a few hours' march away: though the second visit of the ship would have been less of a scramble than the first. It also allowed two days each way for the runners and two days for sending and receiving a message which would have been ample in normal times – and I knew that Sandy and the others, if our runners had found them, would move heaven and earth. But times were not normal. Perhaps our runners, or Sandy's, had been stopped – shot even, by falling into a patrol or an ambush or by being picked off by one of the many German rifles with which the mountains now bristled. Perhaps Sandy's set had broken down – the evil possibilities were many and they proliferated in our thoughts as time passed.

Thus the night of the 2nd of May was hard to endure. There we were, only a few miles from the lonely shore, where, if all had gone well, we should have been stumbling along, for the last time, down those steep crags running down to the sea, hearing the purr of the engine out to sea, flashing our signals, watching for the sailors' white uniforms materialising across the dark of the cove as the creak of the rowlocks grew louder; answering muted hails over the water; then sneaking aboard with our captive and our confederates. (Should the General be piped aboard? After all, we had done our best to maintain standards under trying circumstances . . .) Would Billy's Captain, the bluff and bearded Brian Coleman, be greeting us from the wheel? Soon, as the ship turned about, we would be waving to our dwindling comrades on the rocks as we headed for Africa before the moon got up; then, down to the soft lights of the wardroom, the glow of mahogany and polished brass, the clink of ice. (Pink gin? Whisky? Brandy? *Champagne perhaps . . . ?*) The great silhouette of the island, with the icy watershed of Ida and the White Mountains flashing in the moonlight, would grow smaller through the porthole . . . Red Tabs to greet us the next day at Mersa Matruh, then the flight to Cairo, pointing out to the General the wreckage of all the battles of Montgomery's advance in the desert below, perhaps persuading the pilot to fly in a loop which would embrace El Alamein, landing at Heliopolis; presented arms, goodbye to the General; then, returning in glory to Clusium's royal home with all the delights of Cairo waiting.

This roughly was the talk in English and Greek which accompanied the consoling circuits of the raki bottle among the brambles. Tomorrow night perhaps.

7

Next day everything got much worse. No runner came, and suddenly it would have made no difference if he had. For two hundred of the enemy moved into Saktouria. Our way of escape from the island was blocked. We had to begin all over again.

The southern Messara was stiff with troops; they had moved into Saktouria. Were they going to advance further west and garrison every possible getaway beach? There was only one remedy: for me to leave Billy in charge of the party and head further west, but not beyond touch; to locate our other stations, and if possible, lay hands on one of the sets; and get up-to-date intelligence about the chances for new escape routes. I knew that Billy would be all right with Manoli and Antoni and the rest. The moment I had managed to fix things up, they would make their way westward and join me. The thing was to find a place where a ship could drop anchor and get away in it fast before the Germans moved in; otherwise we might find that all our earths had been stopped. Never has divisibility into three been more longed for: the ability to stay with the party; to sit huddled over a wireless set in touch with Cairo; and to peer down through the rocks at a beach where no Germans were.

After sunset on the 4th of May George and I changed our appearance to that of peaceful rustics, climbed out of our prickly home and set off along the Amari. We dossed down for the night with George's family at Phourphouras. Next morning we followed the more northern of the two Amari ravines; they are separated by the hill of Samitos, bristling with old windmills. To the south, all the pretty villages we had haunted for years – Ay Yanni, Aya

Paraskevi, Khordaki, Ano Meros, Dryes, Vrysses, Kardaki, Gourgouthes, Smiles and Yerakari – flashed along the foothills of Mount Kedros; Ida soared on our right. The transparent spring weather and the buoyant air, the corn, poppies, anemones, asphodels, woods, brooks, the millions of birds – all this, and the opening of a new phase after the staid anxiety of waiting, and above all, being able to move fast and freely by daylight, made everything full of open promise. At least we were moving again.

About midday, there was noise like far-off thunder from the south-east away beyond our hideout; it sounded like a naval battle. We only learnt what it was that evening. The Germans were first bombing and then blowing up with dynamite, house by house in their methodical fashion, the villages of Saktouria, Margarikari, Lokria and Kamares; nobody executed, as far as we could discover. Owing to the disturbed situation, most of the inhabitants were outside their villages, especially at night. The German reasons for this onslaught were that these villages were all hotbeds of bandits, the haunts of the British, hiding places of terrorists, refuges for commandos attacking aerodromes and supply dumps, the hiding places for unnumbered weapons, and the supply point for hundreds of bad men. In Lokria, it said in the official bulletin the next day, there had been no less than ten British officers on the 3rd of May: double the numbers of BLOs in the island. Margarikari, the village of '*the arch-bandit Petrakoyeorgi*', had been destroyed because he had celebrated Easter there with thirty-five of his brigands and all the villagers '*had shown their sympathy with the outlaws*'. Moreover, when he and his men had descended to the village for the funeral of the arch-bandit's mother the whole village had flocked to the church and five priests had sung the requiem. Saktouria was utterly wiped out, the German government said, for the part it had played in the infiltration of arms. (A gun-running trip had landed thirty mule loads of rifles a month before, which had then fanned out all over Crete.) The article ended with another diatribe about the captors of the General: '*Cretans, beware! The edge of the German sword will strike down every one of the guilty men and all the bandits and all the henchmen and hirelings of the English.*'

The reading out loud next day of this communiqué and leading article in the *Parateretes*, the official German Greek-language newspaper, produced the usual reaction of rage and stoicism. So many villages had been burnt, and so many people shot, that these tragedies had, in the end, blotted out all emotions but the thirst for revenge. They had no deterrent effect. Each hecatomb sent a swarm of recruits into the mountains. They were illogical and haphazard, and the shelter of an outlaw on the run or a handful of British stragglers called down the same thunderbolts as the destruction of a squadron of Messerschmitts by sabotage. So, even had the Cretans been disposed to conform, lesser and greater misdeeds were equally dangerous, so, apart from elementary care, it was as well to be killed for a sheep as a lamb.

Some harmless villages, on the same principle as the reprisal shooting of random hostages picked up in the street, were destroyed, but on the whole it was the rebellious villages of the mountains, famous or notorious for years, which bore the brunt; when the time came, any excuse was used. Four months after the end of this story the enemy attacked and destroyed Anoyeia and the Amari villages and as many of the inhabitants as they could capture. The official reason given was that the villages had hidden the General and his captors instead of betraying them. (I learnt the news in hospital in Cairo.) Apart from the shattering nature of the event it was, as one can imagine, deeply upsetting that, in spite of all our insistence in keeping clear of villages and avoiding incriminating the inhabitants, this tragedy should be associated, rightly or wrongly, with the operation.

Certainly, the villagers, luckily for us, had helped us up to the hilt with food, runners, escort, protection and every kind of moral support, as if we had passed through them in procession. It is typical of the general Cretan attitude to their friends that when I got back to the island soon after, they were at pains to play down any reasons for distress. After all, they said, the stricken villages had been deep in resistance from the start, consciously running the risk of German revenge a hundred times over; something was bound to happen some time. The attack on the villages, they went on – the last of a long list of scores of such acts – were the final ones of the German occupation of Crete. They were used as a show of force and terrorism to jar the population into leaving their withdrawal unharried before all the garrisons of the fortress of Crete, which they no longer considered internally defensible, streamed westwards. There, contained by the entire guerrilla strength of the island, they fortified themselves inside the twenty-mile 'Iron Ring' round Canea. The destroyed villages lay in the hinterland along the flank of this line of withdrawal and dominated the ravines through which troops heading westwards would have to pass.

Bearing in mind the long time lag between the operation and its putative aftermath, which was without any precedent in the occupation, these friends thought that the Germans had accepted the line put forward in our letter; all, on principle, would have gone as we had hoped. But, in the months after our departure, by which time our route must have become widely known, details of the operation must have travelled from mouth to mouth until a garbled version reached the wrong ears, and finally those of the enemy. So, when the Germans felt it tactically expedient to strike at some of the villages they considered of particular danger, what pretext – there always had to be one – could be handier than the part these villages had played in spiriting away their General?

These were consoling words; never a syllable of blame was uttered. I listened to them eagerly then, and set them down eagerly now.*

★

* Others are equally determined to stress the link between the reprisals on their villages with the operation; not, however, in any spirit of criticism, but rather because some odd or outlandish aspects of these doings have lodged them in people's memory with a prominence far beyond their real importance. In Crete, singular or untoward events – especially those connected with wars – are often elaborated by hearsay, then in semi-legend, and finally in songs into versions that differ widely from the events that engendered them. This operation is no exception. Some versions stick roughly to the facts, names and places; others feel no such trammels. Mr James Notopoulos, of Harvard University USA, has written (in *Greek, Roman and Byzantine Studies*, Vol. III (1960), 'The

Among the cypresses of Pandanasa George and I ran into a hitch. The Hieronymakis family, we knew, were in touch with at least one of our wireless stations. By ill luck it was about the only village in the region where neither of us had ever been. The Hieronymakis knew all about us, we knew all about them, but we had never met and there was no one to vouch for us. The old men were adamant: '*You say you are Mihali, Mihali who? And who are Siphi (Ralph Stockbridge) and Pavlo (Dick Barnes)? Never heard of them. Tk, tk, tk! Englishmen? But, boys, all the English left Crete three years ago . . .?*'

The white whiskered faces turned to each other for corroboration, beetling brows were raised in puzzlement, blank glances exchanged. They went on calmly fingering their amber beads, politely offering coffee. It was no good raging up and down, gesticulating under the onions and paprika pods dangling from the beams: every attempt to break through was met by identical backward tilts of head with closed eyelids and the placidly dismissive tongue click of the Greek negative. They wouldn't give an inch until they knew (as they say) what tobacco we smoked. We could, after all, be *agents provocateurs*. (There had been rumours in the past of Germans pretending to be English stragglers and a few rare cases of Greek spies, usually recruited by scouring the civilian gaols, who wandered the hills pretending to be resistance people on the run in order to find out and reveal to the enemy for money where guerrillas or arms were hidden. When captured they were shot like vermin. I hoped they didn't think we were such a couple.) They were vague, smiling and inflexible.

This impressive but exasperating wall of security was only broken at last, after two precious hours of deadlock, by the entry of Uncle Stavro Zourbakis from Karines – I think it was him – a friend of

_____

genesis of an oral heroic poem') an interesting pamphlet based on a long metrical sung account of the General's capture recorded in Sphakia, where the names are roughly preserved, but many strange figures occur including a beautiful heroine and a protagonist on horseback. It is an operation in which, as time passes, more and more people, whether they took part in it or not, seem glad to have participated.

us all. Everything dissolved at once – in greetings, recognition, laughter, raki, a crackle of thorns and sizzling in the hearth and the immediate summoning and despatch of runners to the two sets in the north-west.

They had just left when a messenger arrived hot foot from the Amari with a sheaf of letters: one from Billy, saying Sandy's runner had got through at last, dog tired after his hazardous days of travel; and one from Dick Barnes. Sandy's letter had been sent off on the 1st of May. It was now the 5th; our messages to him had left Anoyeia on the 27th; so our two-way traffic with Cairo had taken eight days. His letter, which I have just discovered rummaging through old papers, tattered and nearly illegible, began on the 30th. After kind words about the success of the capture he went on:

We got your messages off at 2.30 today and are waiting for an answer now (7.00 p.m.), when I will send off Drake (code name for one of Sandy's runners) by one route which he knows and the elder of my two, Manolis, by another to confirm. I hope that the boat is on the way. The messages may both get to you in time, but possibly not I fear. As you know, Huns are very thick on the ground. In any case, the message has got there, and I assume you will act if it had. I hope you fixed signals beforehand.

I received an additional wire as follows:

If not rpt not fixed with Paddy already send sigs and timing for Paddys boat all stations. Runner from here may not repeat not reach Paddy before boat due so pse confirm boat will come four following nights as well. The above is probably superfluous but in case you don't get this message and don't go to the spot and the boat comes that night, it still gives everyone a good chance I hope. My second messenger will try and find Tom's haunt and thence you – but I doubt if he can make it. Everyone as you know is being stopped a good deal. Later 1.5.44 we have only just got the answer

(12.30 hours); signal. Boat to Cape Melissa* B.605111 repeat 605111 third, fourth and four following nights. Contact Paddy urgently. All informed. Excellent work. All send congratulations. Acting on instructions your 1/7. (Our 1/7 message was about leaflets and radio broadcasts etc.) Best of luck for rest of trip and love from all here. Sandy.

In spite of the thought that the ship would be coming that night and in vain, for the third time – unless one of the other stations had warned them of the new garrison at Saktouria – Sandy's letter was a great boost, a re-establishment of contact and a proof that Cairo was going all out to help. The news in Dick's letter was out of date too – pre-Saktouria, that is – but it contained the signals to be flashed to the boat on whatever night and near whatever shore it should appear – MK (Monkey King) every ten minutes from 2100 GMT.

The next phase of this story seems even more confused in retrospect than it did at the time. George and I trudged on to the village of Yeni, five miles beyond Pandanasa, a point roughly equidistant from the areas vital to us. We had just learnt that the recent chaos had driven the two stations to new hideouts not far from each other, in the neighbourhood of Kato Valsamonero, south-west of Retimo, north-west of us. The coast from which I hoped we would soon be slipping away lay over the mountains due south; and the party with the General would be advancing to Yerakari – south-east – and hovering in the goat-rocks above that village until the time, the place, and the loved one could all come together at last. The fifteen-odd miles that separates me from each of these regions sounds very little. The whole of Crete is only a fifth the size of Switzerland; but distances, compared to those in Norfolk or the Gobi desert, are nearly as meaningless and these three points all seemed a long way off at the other end of risky labyrinths.

*

* Two miles from Saktouria.

The goat-fold of Zourbovasili, at Yeni, lay in rolling biblical hills. There was a round threshing floor nearby, where George and I could sleep on brushwood with a great circular sweep of vision. This place was to become, during the next three days, the centre of all going and coming of messengers as plans changed and options elapsed. But now, after the scrum of the last few days, it seemed preternaturally quiet in the brilliant moonlight. Ida towered east of us now, Kedros due south; the White Mountains, which had come nearer to us during the day, loomed shining in the west. How empty and still after our huddled mountain life, was this empty silver plateau! A perfect place to watch the moon moving across the sky and chain smoke through the night pondering on the fix we were in and how to get out of it. (How were Billy and the General? Would the Germans move further west along the coast? Was the boat coming, failing a signal flash from teeming Saktouria, at that very moment turning wearily back to Africa for the third time – or the fourth? . . . Now *read on* . . . How I wished I could.) There was not a sound except a little owl in a wood close by and an occasional clank from Vasili's flock.

A letter from Ralph Stockbridge at last! No chance of our joining forces, alas. He was acting as his own operator, his charging engine had gone wrong too, batteries constantly running flat, the people in the area were windy and the caravan that would be needed for the movement of a charging engine and a suitcase wireless, in the low country where he was hiding, far too exposed and full of troops at the moment, was not to be contemplated.

I had feared as much. (How well I knew all those hazards!) It sounded as if he was heading for Priné, an old refuge of ours blown a year ago but perhaps safe again now; these things went in cycles. (Here there would be the staunch backing of Colonel Tziphakis, the defender of Retimo when the parachutists dropped and now the regional head of the resistance movement; and of Uncle George Robola, our protector for years, a tall, white-bearded, and fearless old prophet, smoking his hookas and uttering wise saws among his beehives.)

In more leisurely times, when the Germans were safely ensconced before El Alamein and we were marooned beyond the range of all but an occasional submarine, Ralph would write letters to his colleagues, and elicit answers, in sonnet form. No time for that sort of rot now:

Already sent you two urgent messages with answers to your two previous letters with news and Cairo instructions. I suppose you never got them. Anyway the burning of Saktouria cancels their news. Whether our signals reached Cairo in time to stop boat last night, 5/6 May, heaven knows but I doubt it. Cairo say they broadcast capture of General and that he had reached Cairo, on the 30th and the 1st, and news also published in the press. Leaflets printed at once but not dropped at once because of bad flying weather. Presumably dropped by now.

I wasn't sure whether Ralph meant the leaflets or, metaphorically, the scheme. I hoped, now, the latter, as the less attention drawn at this late hour, the better. '*So sorry can't come and meet you.*' Here follow the reasons I mentioned –

what I suggest is this: Saktouria and Rodakino* are blown. Dick had a boarding party there – and intended evacuation – eight days ago and his signals were answered by machine gun fire from the sea. They have burnt the place down and lots of Huns have been snooping round there. But, at Asi Gonia is Dennis rpt. Dennis. (Captain Dennis Ciclitira.) *He has a set and an operator with him and not much to do and is leaving by next boat which is due I think in about a week in the Preveli area. I suggest you send him a runner then join him and use his set for fixing up boats etc. I will let Dick know too. This is better than runners charging about all over the place with out of date news. I told Cairo all about your situation then my batteries went flat. Damn! I have been up all night charging them. I will also get your signal off about*

* A beach further west.

leaving the Amari and striking w., and tell them to keep me, Dick and Dennis informed of all possibilities and changes and to do their damnedest to get something in, even a destroyer. The signals by the way are M.K. (Monkey King). Obviously you must have a set with you. Dennis is the obvious man. I have got to shift now – these bloody people are scared stiff, so write care of Joe. If you stay where you are do let Dennis know. I will keep in touch. I will also let Dick know. You may want him to join you. If so, could you send a message by mid-day tomorrow. I have already sent you two lots of cigarettes. Here are some more and a map. Love from us all. Ralph.

All this was a bit puzzling but, except for the awful idea of waiting another week before getting away, it could have been worse. Immediately after Ralph's message came another – Costa or Dimitro Koutellidakis with letters from Billy and Manoli. Just before sunset a strong force of Germans had swarmed into the south-east end of the Amari, advanced up the valley beyond Aya Paraskevi, Hordaki and Ay Yanni, exactly where our party was hidden, in fact; then moved in open order down the valley again. It was not clear what they were up to but the whole thing was very fishy.

Guided by Andoni and Michaeli Pattakos – an old friend, always a mass of contradictions and recalcitrance when things were calm and always perfect in times of danger – and the schoolmaster of Koxaré, whose name escapes me, they had managed to get up the side of Mount Kedros in the nick of time, without being seen by the enemy in the falling dusk and without Theophilus catching any tantalising glimpse of his countrymen below. (He had been rather hurt all these days that as far as he could see, General Müller had done so little about rescuing him. If only he had known.) They had scrambled all through the night, making a welcome halt by a hut where they were distilling raki among the streams and the plane trees of Gourgouthes (it must have been the Generali and Katsendoni families, the only inhabitants of the tiny hamlet, probably helped by jovial Sotirios Monahoyios from Khordaki, seldom absent from such doings. During the heroic and hungry

Albanian campaign Sotiri had heard a calf lowing behind the Italian lines, crept through the snow, threw it over his shoulders and dashed back to his own trench under a volley of bullets), and had got to a goat fold above Yerakari, the highest village on the island, while it was still dark. The General had borne up well. At the time of writing, they were both sitting in the sun, hunting their clothes for fleas, Billy said. The night's work had brought the party a big jump closer, and, thanks to the Germans, earlier than we had planned.

Zourbovasili, who had been milking his goats, came over with a foaming cauldron and a huge loaf and we squatted round it with spoons. When he heard about the German thrash through the Amari, he stopped hammering rock salt with a stone and said, 'Eh! General Müller is cross!' Then he sprinkled the salt over the milk and began shaking with silent laughter. 'He had better look out or we will capture him too.'

Dick Barnes's messenger, when he arrived, turned out to be George Psychoundakis, who had first been Xan Fielding's guide and runner for a long time, then mine when I had taken over Xan's area in the west for several months. This youthful Kim-like figure was a great favourite of everyone's, for his humour, high spirits, pluck and imagination and above all the tireless zest with which he threw himself into his task. If anybody could put a girdle round Crete in forty minutes, he could. George, who was a shepherd boy from the great village of Asi Gonia, later wrote a remarkable book about the whole of the occupation, and the resistance movement. I translated it from his manuscript and it was published, under the title *The Cretan Runner* (John Murray, London), with great success. It is a wonderful book, which I hotly recommend to anyone interested in these things. His account of those particular days is moving, very lively and funny, and always true.

This extraordinary boy not only brought a letter from Dick – but, by speeding over the whole of Retimo and setting a swarm of lesser runners in motion, he helped many of our problems on their way to solution. He found Leftheri Papayanakis from the village of Akhtounda, just inland from the stretch of coast due south of us from which I hoped we could find a German-free beach to get away. A garrison had long been established at Preveli Monastery; but what about the little cove of Karamé, on the steep southern slope of Mount Kedros? Leftheri was to spy out the land and report. Next George found and brought Yanni Katsias, for whom I had been searching, a great tough, free-booting giant like a Kazantzakis hero who knew every stone, spring, hole and foot-path of the southern region mountains. Up to the neck for years in the old feuding and raiding life of these ranges, and a veteran of flock-rustling forays, he was a perfect man to guide us over old hidden tracks and keep us out of sight and away from harm. He came loping over the hills to join us with his wary and wolf-like gait. Extremely good-looking, and armed at all points, a heavily fringed turban redundantly shaded a face already by no means open; and his size and strength was such that the rifle which was never out of his hand, carried loosely at the point of balance, seemed reduced to the size and weight of a twig. A better friend than foe; luckily we had always been very fond of each other.

Dashing away to the north-west again, to the crevasse at Dryade where their wireless set was, again George returned next morning with Dick Barnes himself, an utterly convincing Cretan in boots, kerchief and shaggy cape. I feared the same difficulties about transport, while everything was still upside down, prevented his set from coming any closer; he would have had to go off the air for a day, too, just when we needed it most. Much better to leave it *in situ* with the Changebug⋆ flying to and fro like Ariel. Should no beach be suitable due south he was in favour, unlike Ralph, of fixing up something in the Rodakino area about three days' march westwards.

The situation over there sounded confused. During recent months, the guerrilla bands had been expanding like a crop of dragon's teeth. A week earlier Dick's signals out to sea had been answered by machine-gun bursts and actual mortar bombs from a

⋆ [George.]

German coastal craft. Then a party of Germans had marched into Rodakino and started burning the village. The Rodakiniot bands opened fire on them, and then waylaid a reinforcement which was going to join them. Then waiting till they were at very close range, they wiped out the lot, except for two prisoners. The other Germans fled from the half-burnt village leaving the place, for the moment at any rate, free of the enemy. If only it were a bit closer! I was getting very anxious lest our whereabouts became too widely known as the days passed, but if we couldn't get away due south, the west began to beckon with a steadily increasing glow. Everything depended on the results of Leftheri's reconnaissance.

This reunion with Dick – like many occasions in occupied Crete when one wasn't actually dodging the enemy – became the excuse for a mild blind. '*Mr Pavlo and I set off to Yeni*,' writes George Psychoundakis in his book,

where we found Mr Mihali (me) and Uncle Yanni Katsias. We sat there till the evening and the sun set. Yanni took us to the east side of the village where they brought us some food and first rate wine and our Keph (well-being) was great. The four of us were soon singing. Mr Mihali sang a sheep-stealing couplet to the tune of Pentozali, *which went:*

> *Ah, Godbrother, the night was dark*
> *For lamb and goat and dam, Sir,*
> *But when we saw the branding mark,*
> *We only stole the ram, Sir.*

The ram – the head of the flock – meant the General. It was a couplet he'd made up in the style of the old Cretan mantinada which runs:

> *Ah Godbrother, we couldn't see,*
> *The night was black and dirty,*
> *But when we saw the branding mark,*
> *We only rustled thirty.*

(It is a satirical couplet about a sheep thief, suddenly finding out that the animals he plans to lift belong to his god-brother; but seeing his god-brother's earmark he takes only thirty instead of the whole flock. It's all a bit obtuse and sounds rather boastful.)

Yanni had shot an enormous hare in the afternoon, which he had cooked with oil and onions. He had come to be very fond of the Changebug as he had rescued his two small children from a village fired by the Germans a few months earlier, by running across a whole mountain range with them piggy-back. We sat late in the moonlight, emptying the demijohn. It was just what we all needed to forget the stress and anxiety of the situation. George got back with news that all was going well with the other party. I slept properly for the first time for many nights, still vaguely thinking about the problematical arrival of the boat, but, thanks to that first rate-wine, at one remove. (It's my delight on a shiny night and the signals are Monkey King.) Dick and George Psychoundakis returned to their den next day.

Excellent communications had now been established. On the night of the 7th, the party with the General moved by an easy night march to Patsos, which was only two or three hours away from me. They were being fed and guarded by George Harocopos and his family. (George, a thoughtful and well-read boy, later to become a gifted journalist, was the son of a very poor, but very brave and kind family, all of whom had been great benefactors to the wandering British.) All was going according to plan. If only the news from the coast turned out well!

The news, when it came through at last, was bad. Leftheri had had a terribly bad time clambering about both chasms and cliffs; not only had the garrison at Preveli been doubled, but a strong German contingent had been landed by sea, presumably from Timbaki, at Keramé – the very place from which I had hoped we might escape. There were still one or two beaches which might just be used, but there was a lot of going and coming of Germans all along the coast. It was very sinister. This activity in a region so remote and desolate where they had never before set foot, coupled with the German sweep down the Amari valley, had an ominous look. Leftheri had left a man down there to keep his eye on things and send warnings of anything new. A tiny cove called Limni seemed the only likely place still left. Off went a runner to Dick with the sad tidings, and I sent Yanni Katsias to the west to see what was happening at Rodakino.

Jack Smith-Hughes, in charge of the Cretan section of Force 133 (SOE) in Cairo, must have been having an anxious time. It was only since we had regained contact that I fully realised how well we were being backed up; these goat folds and threshing floors seemed so remote from [SOE headquarters at] Rustum buildings and the traffic of the Sharia Kasr el Ani!

A runner from Dick suddenly arrived with an exciting and disturbing signal: George Jellicoe and a strong contingent of SBS Raiding Forces were landing at Limni beach on the night of the 9th/10th with orders to contact us by hook or by crook. They were bringing their own wireless kit, and fighting their way if necessary to organise the evacuation as soon as possible in collusion with me, from some other beach. No signals were included in the message, so it looked as if they were landing blind, in order not to jeopardise things by trying to combine this crash landing in Crete with the more delicate business of transporting and guarding the General.

This was terrific. George Jellicoe was – still is – a resilient, unconventional and infectious compendium of energy, intelligence and humour, and gifted with a great flair for attack and unrattled inventiveness in trouble. Better still, he had raided Crete two years earlier, having landed with three French officers and a commando force. They'd blown up a vast quantity of German planes and fuel, but, uniquely in Crete, a traitor had given them away to the Germans and loss and capture had bedevilled their almost miraculous withdrawal; so he knew just how dangerous these things could be. Since then he and his unit had been wreaking havoc behind enemy lines all over the place. I was just beginning to revel in the thought of this magical ending to our troubles when a message came from Leftheri

Kallithounakis's man at the coast: '*Germans just moved into Limni.
Keep away!*'

George was due to arrive next evening, so they must already
be at sea. I sent off a runner to Dick urging him to bombard
Cairo with warnings to be transmitted to the ship; if there were
a breakdown, as there very often was, George and his boys
would be landing in the middle of a reception committee. The
only solution was to rejoin Billy and the General at once, send
them on further west with a strong escort in the hope of
evacuation later near Rodakino, then to collect a dozen men
with guns – there was no dearth of these, luckily – and dash
down to the sea, and then, after dark, split into two parties and
hang about in the rocks as close as we could to the Germans.
When we heard the ship approaching we would start a diversion in the opposite direction which would either warn George
and his raiders not to land, or, with a bit of luck and shouts
across the water, guide them onto a part of the shore from
which the enemy had been lured. Then, before the Germans
could realise what on earth was going on, we could all hare
over the mountain, hide in a cave for the next day, then at
night, discreetly join the sedater western progress of the General.
(It is amazing how much confusion a few people can cause in
the dark.)

Judging by George Psychoundakis' reaction when I outlined
the scheme to him, I foresaw great difficulty in getting anyone
to remain with the General at all. Manoli wouldn't like it; nor
would Billy, nor would the Antonies, nor would Gregori . . .
George said we might draw lots for one person to stay with the
General tomorrow night . . . this chat accompanied our moonlight
march over the hills to Patsos. George's final solution was to put
the General in a comfortable cave, then roll a huge boulder into
the entrance for one night while we all streamed south to guide
o Lordos Tzelliko and his amphibian thugs ashore.

I need hardly say that this brief project came to nothing. The
warning message got through allright and just as Billy and I were

arranging the details, a message arrived saying the operation was postponed for several days. Rodakino sounded a likelier solution every moment. We would go west that night. Of course it was better so, but a bit of an anticlimax all the same.

8

The party, when I found them, were star-scattered about a tumble-down stone hut shaded by a clump of tall plane trees and a beetling rock with a waterfall and a deep pool. George Harocopos and his old father and his pretty little sister were looking after them in this Daphnis and Chloë décor. Billy records that, as the party had been there two days and there were many mouths to fill and also a chance that George, the mainstay of the household, might leave us, I tried to force some sovereigns on Uncle Evthymios, his father. This was a scene that often happened. Two years before, I had sent five sovereigns with a covering letter saying, 'Herewith for cigarettes', to Aleko Kokonas, the schoolmaster of Yerakari, who had been ruining himself and his friends in support of British stragglers. The coins came back next day with a note, '*Thanks Mihali, but I'm a non-smoker.*'

It was nearly always the same story. We just managed to pay our headquarters expenses, but little else, except occasionally helping people left in the lurch from sudden death or disaster. The same applied to all this lordly talk on every page about sending runners off all over the land. They, like everyone else in this story, were unpaid volunteers who worked as they did because they felt honour bound to do so. We were allies and there was no more to be said. That is why all the references to '*Hirelings of the English*' in German communiqués were so ludicrously wide of the mark. They were as mistaken as their references, in the context of guerrilla activity, to '*Communists*' and '*Bolsheviks*'. The only communist contributions to the Cretan resistance were their attempts – for which, fortunately, they were too late in the field:

all that was worthwhile in the island had been absorbed years before by the non-political EOK movement⋆ – to disrupt the resistance for post-war political ends as they managed to do with great skill in the rest of Europe.

'*Good morning, General. How are you?*' '*Ah, Good morning, Major. We missed you.*' We might have been in a drawing room. Billy told me that the General's mood had been alternating between morose depression and comparative cheerfulness. They had had a slight tiff, now made up, at the time of the village burnings. I think they were kept at a further distance from each other than they would normally have been by the Potsdam–Carthusian French which was their only medium; it was too rickety a bridge for all but the most tentative exchanges.

The General had become very fond of Manoli; and Manoli had the impression that he might try to escape; he was keeping a sharper lookout, especially at night. For some reason George filled him with misgiving – rather strangely, for George had a very kind nature; I think the memory of the closeness of George's dagger during our ride through Herakleion had left a deep trace. As a German, the General had at first been an object of horror to all of our party; as a human being, in the higgledy-piggledy proximity of recent days, their feelings were guarded but favourable on the whole. My tentative feelings of sympathy had started, I think, with the ode to Thaliarchus, on Mount Kedros, looking towards Mount Ida, and I have an idea that it was returned, though we neither referred to it for the same reason. At any rate, we all thanked our stars that, as things had turned out, our prisoner was not General Müller and a notorious war criminal: life would have become insupportable.

It was easy to gather that the General was far from being an eager Nazi or admirer of Hitler. I asked him about war crimes; he said he knew that there had been terrible deeds in the Ukraine and that elsewhere '*many things had happened which ought not to*

⋆ [Ethniki Organosi Kritis (National Organisation of Crete); centrist resistance organisation.]

have happened.' In my queer role of half captor, half host, I felt rather loath to press him on awkward themes; after all, we weren't interrogation officers. He was amazed by our close relationship with the Cretans. I explained about the feelings prevailing between England and Greece since the Albanian campaign, and even long before, and I told him, as well as I could, and as far as discretion allowed, the reasons for the present *Husarenstück*; he nodded slowly and pensively and thought there might be something in it. I asked him about Germany's allies on the Russian front and was very surprised by the answer. By far the best, he said, were the Romanians, who fought like demons – '*wie Teufel*' (not, perhaps, it occurred to me, so much for ideological reasons, as from ancient and atavistic fears, all too justified, about the fate of Bessarabia). Next came the Italians, who had been, to his great astonishment, very good indeed. As for the Hungarians, it was, he said, as though they had no heart in it. The Russian campaign sounded a nightmare. He reminisced a lot about the Great War; then the conversation ranged over many things.

Our sudden change of plan had produced a momentary lull. Once more, there was a great feeling of strangeness about these recumbent hours of smoking and talk beside the shady waterfall. I had an inkling that, even in more cheerful times for him, the General had rather a solitary nature through which ran a dash of melancholy; though there were plenty of reasons at the moment for the deep sighs which recurred both in his talk and in moments of silence.

Our way westward over the plateau of Yious was our familiar east-to-west route over the narrowest part of western Crete. '*Our sun is rising,*' George had said as we set off at moonrise. It was a favourite saying in these nocturnal journeys. '*Off we go,*' Manoli said, '*Anthropoi tou Skotous.*' This phrase, '*men of Darkness!*', was a cliché that often cropped up in German propaganda when referring to people like us, and we had eagerly adopted it. We were off, I hoped, on the last lap of our journey. Diana's foresters. Minions of the moon.

Among the rocks and arbutus clumps there was an ice-cold spring which was said to bestow the gift of immortality. We all lay on our faces and lapped up as much as we could hold. I told the General about the property of the water. He leant down from the saddle of his mule and asked urgently for a second mug. Among the trees outside the hamlet of Karines, a bit further on, Uncle Stavros Zourbakis, forewarned to make sure the coast was clear, was waiting with Kiria Eleni, his high-spirited wife (a crack shot with a rifle) and their daughter Popi – our hosts and guardian angels on scores of journeys – with a tray of raki glasses and peeled walnuts. We swigged them down and went on our way munching. Then the plateau sank into a deep valley, a danger point, as the only north–south motor road ran along the bottom between the big garrisons of Spili in the south and Armenoi and Retimo in the north. (A few months after this, Antoni Zoidakis, escorting Tom, fell badly wounded in a gun fight with a German patrol at exactly this point. They tied him by the feet to the back of a truck and drove full speed to Armenoi, four miles to the north, and left poor Antoni's body beside the road, as a warning to the guerrillas, mangled and stone-dead.)

Men with guns whistled from the rocks and when we answered ran down to meet us and shepherd the party across the perilous highway. Others joined us out of the moonlight as we climbed into the conical hills where Fotinou is perched. Suddenly there was an alarm of a German patrol approaching directly ahead. Our party, by now quite large, fanned out along a ridge and lay waiting. Billy and Manoli and I seized the General from his saddle and flung him and ourselves down among the heather, and peered down at the approaching figures. Billy reports that I said, '*If it comes to a scrap we've got them taped.*' Luckily it was only another contingent of our growing escort. There was relief and laughter.

By the time we got to the grove of Scholari outside Fotinou, we were very numerous indeed. Most of the troop was composed of old Uncle Stavro Peros and his eighteen sons and their descendants with several members of the Tsangarakis and Alevizakis families as well. Andoni, the youngest of the Peros brothers, had just contracted a dynastic match with the daughter of a family with whom the Peros tribe had been locked in discord for generations; so an atmosphere of concord and rejoicing reigned in the hills. Very sadly, we lost Grigori Chnarakis from the party. Some more of the Russian deserters, like those of Kastamonitza, had fetched up in Fotinou – Billy had formed the idea of returning and organising them into a guerrilla group. So, as Grigori was not planning to leave with us for Egypt, he was going to guide them back to the east to join the others. We were all sorry to see him go. (One of the Russians, Piotr, much older than the rest, was too ill to walk. We found a mule for him in the hopes of getting him to Egypt.)

The General was an object of wonder to all our companions. They couldn't feast their eyes on him enough. The atmosphere was rather that of the Sheriff of Nottingham brought captive to Sherwood Forest.

All through the following night the country changed gradually from the gently airy plateau, south of Retimo, which divides the Aegean from the Libyan sea and links the two great massifs of Crete, into steeper slopes, more precipitous ravines, a world which grows wilder and shaggier with every advancing mile. Mount Ida, far far away now in the east, gleamed remotely under the rising moon while ahead of us the watersheds that divide the nomes of Retimo and Canea rumbled across the middle distance like the warning notes of the huge thunderstorms of the White Mountains which ran wild into the sky beyond them: a flashing pandemonium of pallor and shadow which rages away westwards in spikes and landslides and rotting cliffs that overhang gorges flashing and zigzagging like forked lightning across the planetary chaos. Echoing ravines, as narrow as corridors, dropped into the darkness to soar once more to the great summits of Sphakia and away westwards again to the ultimate, ibex-haunted wilderness of Selino. The Turks never held the region in complete subjection; vendettas, in which whole villages could be embroiled, still raged between families; and the rustling and counter-rustling of flocks filled many of those ranges with perils that had nothing to do with the present war. The outskirts of this tremendous region now swallowed us up.

At a hut near Alones Yanni Katsias was waiting, with two very wild-looking boys whose appearance aptly epitomised the mood of the approaching mountains, and our old escort turned back to Fotinou. We were joined too – he suddenly materialised out of the trees further on, as though instinct had summoned him there – by Eleftherios Alevizakis, son of Father John, the brave and saint-like priest of Alones. (Father John, in spite of the capture and execution of one of his sons, had sheltered and befriended many of us for years. It was with great difficulty that after endless raids on his village we had persuaded this tall, bearded and spectacled figure, one of the most outstanding of the resistance, to go to Cairo – at least till things had blown over a bit.)

A mishap occurred on this long night's march: the girth of the General's mule broke and sent his rider tumbling down a steep precipice. We chased after him; we thought at first that one of his shoulder blades was damaged; we arranged a sling and after a while the pain seemed to go. But his right arm remained in a sling for the rest of the journey. It was an anxious moment.

Outside the little village of Vilandredo we were met by kind and enthusiastic Stathi Loukakis and his brother, yet another Stavro. (We were back in the god-brother network. I had spent my first Cretan months nearby and Xan Fielding and I had christened Stathi's little daughter, another Anglia; which was why we had headed for Vilandredo.) He led us all, dog-tired and woe-begone, to a built-up cave that clung to the mountainside like a martin's nest. It was only to be reached by the clambering ascent of a steep ladder of roots and rocks – up which our disabled captive could only be hoisted by many hands and slow stages.

But, once we were inside, everything took a really promising turn: a booted and turbaned and heavily bearded figure with his goatskin cloak about him lay fast asleep in the corner of the cave. It was our colleague Dennis Ciclitira, no less. His wireless set, we had learnt from god-brother Stathi, was only just up the valley at

Asi Gonia. Yanni Katsias had told me, at our rendezvous near
Alones, through teeth clenched like a portcullis in the south-west
Retimo and Sphakian way – it turns all their Ls into Rs, one of
the many odd characteristics of the local accent – that he and his
two chaps had explored the Rodakino beach: there was not a
single German anywhere near. I hardly dared to think of it, but
as we all tucked the General up as snugly as possible I couldn't
help feeling that things must go right at last.

At first things really did look promising. As it turned out, however,
new contingencies churned everything up in a tangle which takes
a little unravelling.

Dennis, who had come to Vilandredo to help us, set off for
Asi Gonia. (This village – George Psychoundakis' home – is a
great stronghold the other side of a wide valley running north,
a place with an old guerrilla tradition and now the centre of an
important and well-disciplined band under Kapitan Petraka
Papadopetrakis (codename 'Beowulf', from his fair whiskers and
general bearing), an old friend.) Dennis would do all he could to
hasten the ship's advent and keep in touch.

Rumours of a German descent on the region had prompted
Stathi to conceal us in such a cramped and precarious eyrie the
night before; next morning all seemed serene: we climbed up to
a commodious and beautiful ledge of rock where the General was
consoled for the agonies of the ascent by the coloured blankets
and the cushions spread there under the leaves by my god-brother
and Stavro (an old drinking companion of mine) and by the marvellous banquet of roast sucking pig and *kalitsounias* – crescent-shaped
mizithra* croquettes – and the wicker demijohn of magnificent old
wine which was waiting. Stathi was a great *bon viveur* and a paragon
of kindness and generosity as well as being Kapetanios of an armed
band. His eager blue eyes kindled with delight to see us demol-
ishing his feast. He hoped (and so did we) that we could lie up
here in luxury until we slipped off over the hill to the boat.

* [Soft cheese.]

There was a rushing stream hard by and sweet-smelling herbs all round us and the trees were full of nightingales. We banqueted and slept and talked and sang. The sun set through the surrounding peaks and as we lolled exulting on the soft rugs under the moon and the stars, forever plied with fresh marvels by the two brothers, who sped to and from the village like kindly djinns, this sudden change in our affairs seemed to all of us as magical as the sudden transportation to paradise for beggars in a Persian story.

But next morning, two hundred Germans detrucked in Argyroupolis, the road terminus less than an hour away.

We clambered back to our first cave. After dark my god-brothers were leading us to a still safer hideout when, with a crashing of branches and a shout, the General – a dim silhouette now in the midst of our party – lost his balance and fell into the void below: a painful drop of several yards through the undergrowth. Climbing down, we prised him laboriously back on to the footpath again. Utter depression succeeded the fury unleashed by this new mishap.

But the heaviest cross we had to bear during the troubles of the next twenty-four hours was Piotr the Russian. With great difficulty we'd found him a mule for the march from Fotinou, and whenever possible we supplied him with comforts and atten-tion – Stathi brought him special soups and covering and we all did what we could to help him. Not only was there never a murmur of thanks but the only syllables he uttered were sneering words of scorn and hatred about both the English and the Greeks. He was a middle-aged man of repulsive ugliness and filthy habits; how unlike the two jolly Russian deserters who had celebrated Easter with us! The Cretans had never clapped eyes on a creature so bestial; nor had we.

Slowly, the pity we all felt for an ally in distress turned to disgust and loathing. There was something darkly comic about the total abjection of our new companion. I think it was Manoli who first nicknamed him Pendamorphi, the Five Times Lovely One – the beautiful princess in Greek fairy tales. This inspiration made things a bit better but it was Pendamorphi who now slowed

Patrick Leigh Fermor as a Cretan mountaineer, Kyriakosellia, 30 January 1943. 'The apt epitome of a long and reckless tradition of mountain feud, guerilla, and armed revolt . . .'

Xan Fielding, Kyriakosellia, 30 January 1943

Arthur Reade at Gournes before the raid on the beehive huts, 24 January 1943

Leigh Fermor's team at Hordaki, on the run after the raid at 'the Eagle's Nest', Fourfouras, early May 1943. Leigh Fermor (*front left*), Niko Soures (*behind*), Matthew White (*top left*), Aristides Paradisianos (*centre*), Yanni Tsangarakis (*centre front*), George Tyrakis holding a sheep's scapula (*front right*)

Leigh Fermor and Yanni Tsangarakis at Hordaki, early May 1943. 'Yanni . . . my best friend in Crete . . . the best and hardest worker we have ever had here.'

Leigh Fermor, George Tyrakis and Athanasios Bourdzalis planning the escape route, 20 April 1944. A glance at the map at once indicated the vast bulk of Mount Ida . . . a familiar refuge to most of us, but, to the enemy, a daunting and perilous labyrinth haunted by guerrilla bands and outlaws.'

Leigh Fermor at the hideout at Kastamonitza, 20 April 1944.
'We passed the time talking and reading out loud.'

Moss and Leigh Fermor in battledress, 20 April 1944

The abduction party at Xylouris' hideout, 28 April 1944, Moss and Leigh Fermor in German uniform. *Clockwise from top left:* Emmanouil Paterakis (Manoli); Leigh Fermor; Moss; George Tyrakis; Nikolaos Komis (Nikos); Antoni Papaleonidas; Efstratios Saviolakis (Stratis); Grigori Chnarakis

Manoli Paterakis and George Tyrakis at Xylouris' hideout, 28 April 1944

Restaging the abduction, 1946. 'There was only one good place for an ambush: the point where the steeply banked minor road from Archanes joined the main road from the south . . .'

Leigh Fermor and Moss resting at Xylouris' hideout, 28 April 1944

Moss, General Kreipe and Leigh Fermor at Xylouris' hideout, 28 April 1944

At the snowline on Mount Ida, 29 April 1944. 'The last stunted mountain cedar vanished, leaving us in a stricken world where nothing grew and a freezing wind threatened to blow us off our feet. Then deep snow turned every step into torment.'

Leigh Fermor handing over Kreipe in Cairo, 17 May 1944. 'The General's behaviour was most friendly and helpful throughout and he put up with the hardships of mountain travel and rough living with fortitude.'

Captor and prisoner reunited in Athens, 1972. 'We had both drunk at the same fountains long before; and things were different between us for the rest of our time together.'

up and endangered our progress, not the long-suffering General. I detected an occasional look of reproach in the glances of my companions; they were quite right. His adoption was an act of true folly which deserved to bring the whole operation to disaster.

We changed our hideout several times in accordance with the German movements. One party had headed to Asi Gonia; another plunged along the valley to Vilandredo itself. It was one of those times of hide and seek which, after hiding in the branches of a clump of cedars a year before while an enemy battalion thrashed through the tree trunks below, Xan and I called Oakapple Days, on the analogy of Charles II's flight after the Battle of Worcester.

At one point in this agitated interlude a boy got through from Asi Gonia with a message about an impending boat at Rodakino; the time, place and signals were to be confirmed later. This buoyed us up in our troubles which began to multiply. Apart from the General's accidents and Piotr's distemper, all our footgear was disintegrating; the torn shoes of Miki and Elias had almost ceased to exist; poor Antoni Papaleonidas was stricken down by terrible pains in the back: sometimes he had to drop behind, but he always caught us up again with apologetic smiles. A mysterious cramp seemed to have settled semi-permanently in my right forearm.

At one dark crevasse – our third cache – we were skulking and shuddering, waiting for Stathi and Stavro to come. They arrived, several hours after they had planned, with baleful news that a hundred Germans had surrounded the village so that nobody had been able to get out or in. They were asking, Stathi told us in a whisper, looking towards the huddled figure of our prisoner, for General Kreipe. Then they left.

9

'*Well, Herr Major, how are the plans for our departure progressing?*' By now the General had become as solicitous for the success of our departure as we were.

'*Wunderbar, Herr General! We're leaving!*'

It was true, the order of release, or the promise of it, had come through. The German drive through the Asi Gonia mountains had driven Dennis to earth and put his set momentarily off the air. But messages from Cairo were beamed now to all stations and when the great news came through, Dick himself, hearing of our local troubles, and making a dash clean across the nome of Retimo, reached our cheerless grotto long after dark. The boat would put in at a beach near Rodakino at 22 hours on the night of the 14th /15th May — '*10 o'clock tomorrow night!*' It was in exactly a day from now. We would only just be able to manage it.

The thing was to get the main party to the coast under cover of darkness. I sent Billy off with George and the others and Yanni Katsias and his two wild boys by a short route which would bring them by daybreak to a place where they could wait for us. The General, Manoli and I would go by a much longer and safer way, where the mountains were so steep and deserted that, with a cloud of scouts out, we could move by day without much danger. Unfortunately it was too steep and uneven for a mule so the General would have to go on foot. But the sky was clear and there would be a bright moon and starlight. Yanni would warn the Rodakino bands that we were heading for their mountains and ask some of them to come and meet us. The Krioneritis mountains which we were to cross are not one of the highest ranges of Crete, but they are among the steepest and are certainly the worst going. They are bare and, except for an occasional thistle or thornbush or sea squill, as empty of vegetation as a bone yard; the place is ringed with craters and fractured into a jigsaw of deep crevasses; worst of all there is not a path or even a flat square foot in the whole of this wilderness. The region is a never-ending upside-down harrow armed with millions of limestone sickles and daggers and yataghans.

Sustained perhaps by the thought of an end to his ordeal, the General tackled this *via crucis* with scarcely a groan. Helped by Manoli and me when he stumbled and then by the guerrillas that shimmered like ghosts out of the vacancy, he moved across the landscape in a sort of trance. But, tormenting as our journey was, the dazzle of the moon and, when it set, of a blaze of stars that was nearly as bright, undermined this commotion of rock and then, by a planetary device in collusion with the optical tricks of which, at some moments, Crete seems to be composed – involving manipulated reflection and focus, levitation, geometrical shifts and a dissolving of solids balanced by a solidification of shadow – filled the hollow, then porous and finally transparent island under foot with lunar and stellar properties and, while hoisting it several leagues in the air, simultaneously, with moves as quiet as an opening gambit followed by those advances of knights and bishops, fast and stealthy as grandmother's steps, which lead to penultimate castling and a sudden luminous checkmate, regrouped all the mountain tops of Crete within touching distance. The valleys and foothills had dropped away from this floe of triangles; they drifted in the windless cold starlight with the pallor, varying with their distance, of ice or ivory.

How did the Five Times Lovely One get across this beautiful inferno? I can't remember, but I know that I saw him later on the ship sitting among the tackle with lack lustre eyes and unadjusted dress. He was beyond walking. I think a burly, unsqueamish Samaritan took him on his back. He went aboard later slung from a pole between two hefty guerrillas. Meanwhile my right arm felt stranger and stranger; it was quite painless, but I found I could neither straighten it nor raise it very high.* Perhaps it was just as well we were going away.

The sun rose behind Mount Ida and by the time it was up about twenty guerrillas were padding along beside us. They were all from the Rodakiniot band of the Kapitans Yanna, Kotsiphis and Khombitis. Like a number of their men, these were old friends from my time in their region, but I hadn't seen most of them for a year and a half.

A studied but dashing nonchalance marks the way people dress on the Retimo–Canea border and in spite of the patched boots and torn clothing of mountain life, most of them were dressed in black shirts, their fringed turbans rakishly looped and their cartridge clips buckled tightly round their mulberry-sashed middles. The looks are splendid hereabouts. There was a surprising lot of fair hair and grey eyes. There is also an aquiline, rather Hispano-Mauresque fineness in many of the features which may spring from the Saracenic occupation, especially along this southern shore, a thousand years ago; eyebrows like pen strokes, and eyes that blaze out like lamps. A mixture of relaxed ease and bohemianism, coupled with reckless alacrity and high spirits, stamps their bearing. They are ready for anything. At the moment an infectious feeling of elation filled them; it was caused by the rout of the Germans a fortnight earlier. The situation in these hills was an odd one: the Germans had burnt down Rodakino; several months before,

---

* This curious ailment got worse. Two days after landing my right leg was attacked by the same trouble. Within a week I was in hospital stiff as a plank. It went on for three months; then gradually unclenched and vanished as mysteriously as it had come. It was at first thought to be infantile paralysis, then 'rheumatic infection of the joints', incurred by sleeping out for years in wet clothes. Another doctor diagnosed the thing as psychosomatic. He thought that, at times like the successive postponements and frustrations and dangers of the last days, one is more anxious than one realises and somehow, when the subconscious anxiety relaxes a bit, nature steps in indignantly. I don't know. I was back in Crete in the autumn, completely allright and, touch wood, there's never been a hint of a return. I only mention this because of its oddity: a Cretan friend said, 'You must have been Eyed.'

after the bands of Manoli Bandouvas and Manoli Yanna, with Tom and Xan, had come into headlong collision with a strong body of the enemy and driven them off with loss, the Germans had blown up Kallikratis, the next biggest village in the area, with the result that the Germans had no sanctions left and the guerrillas moved about the forbidden zones of the coast, in full sight and range of the German garrison below, completely unmolested. There was no more to lose.

A few hours later we were gazing down at the point where these Germans, fortunately about two miles from our intended point of exit, lived in a strongly defended barbed wire perimeter. (Our march, till the reunion with Billy's party in the middle of the morning, had taken thirteen hours. It was considered a great feat.) Billy and the others had arrived at our tryst – a jut of the mountains commanding the entire coast – just before dawn. There was a great feeling of excitement in the air. The main body of the enemy were a mile further west. We watched the outpost directly beneath us as they moved about their pen at normal garrison tasks. Suddenly they all seemed to be bounding across an open space in an extending line which began to shrink at the other end. I asked Manoli for the binoculars. He looked through them, laughed and handed them to me. Billy adjusted his and when we saw they were only playing leapfrog, songs burst simultaneously from our lips. The General looked down a long time and handed back the glasses with one of his deep sighs. I don't think he was thinking of rescue. It was too late now, and, with all those black-clad guerrillas lying smoking and quietly talking among the rocks with their guns beside them, too remote a contingency. I think the sigh, and the resigned smile and the shrug that followed, meant that those minute figures below were the last of the German Army he would see until the war was over. He said, not sarcastically, '*You must be feeling pleased.*'

But I wasn't, not altogether. Billy and I both felt that all would go well this time. The Rodakino captains had done us proud: long before the ship was due, there would be eighty or a hundred well-armed men in the mountains to shut up the passes inland and to swoop down the mountainside, should there be trouble at the last moment; they could hold those Thermopylean narrows between the sea and the mountains against a whole regiment.

But Crete is always difficult to leave; it was especially so now. The coast retreated east and west in a score of towering folds and each succeeding cape, in the clarity of this lens-light air, was as precise in detail as the rocks where we lay; they only dimmed as they sank under the surface. Visible there for many fathoms, they plunged headlong into those peacock-blue soundings to depths of the Libyan sea so far from the water line as the great tangled watersheds behind us. Only the island of Gavdos broke the glitter of the expanding sea beyond. The cliffs below were a descending jungle of thyme, rockrose, heather, myrtle, arbutus and verbena, oleanders marked the pebble and boulder strewn torrent beds and the air was loaded with the smell of herbs. Who would exchange all this, and nightingales and the sounds of goatfolds and herdsmen calling across the gulfs of air, and the echo of shots along empty gorges, for tram bells, jacarandas, carrion crows and muezzins?

And the Cretans? There has been more than a hint in these pages of their kindness and generosity and of that aspect of Cretan life which suddenly gives the phrase 'Brotherhood in arms' such meaning; there were many things to make one sorry to leave, even for so short an absence as I hoped mine would be, from the struggle that was afoot; not through indispensability, far from it; but because some infectious property of the contest and many links of friendship had involved us in it during the last years, to a point where difference of race meant little. We were up to the neck in a singular phenomenon with most unusual beginnings.

When the Germans invaded Crete, their armies had just defeated the whole of Europe, except – thanks, perhaps, to the fluke of the Channel's existence – England. Peace had been signed on the mainland where the whole Cretan division was now marooned. Logically the civilian population could have been expected to remain inactive while the professionals – the British, Commonwealth and a small number of Greek troops – fought it out with the invaders. But, to the great astonishment of both sides, all over the island bodies of Cretans – villagers, shepherds, old men, boys, monks and priests and even women, without any collusion between them or master plan or arms or guidance from the official combatants – rose up at once and threw themselves on the invaders with as little hesitation as if the German war machine were a Basha's primitive expedition of janissaries armed with long guns and scimitars. They had not had a second's doubt about what they should do.

This atavistic reaction to the violation of their island – comparable, in spirit and on a smaller scale, to the vigour of Greece's automatic reaction to the Italian invasion when they flung the invaders back into Albania and nearly into the sea – was reinforced by another instinct; the compulsion to lend a hand to a friend in the lurch (*'Listen to that! Our allies, who have come a long way over the sea, are fighting the enemy in our mountains. Come on!'*). This phenomenal response to a challenge may have had little tactical or strategic result; how could it, when the official defenders were themselves driven out? But the psychological and moral results were enormous. (Crete differs from the rest of the world at many points and critics who try to evaluate cause and effect there, especially in military matters, are soon astray.) The German revenge for the Cretans' share in the battle was an immediate holocaust of burning and shooting. From that moment there was no looking back and the skull and crossbones was run up the mast. The resistance movement had come into being as the first parachutist touched ground.

During the next year it grew in strength, cohered and ramified all over the island through the organising of the shelter and the guidance to safety of Allied stragglers, and soon in working with emissaries sent in from the free world outside to help them. This spontaneous growth, rooted in fighting the enemy and in works of mercy to their friends, involved all that was good in the island, all the natural leaders, all that was courageous, unselfish and wise. Political differences were sunk; there was no struggle for power; apart from the determination to help win the war, there was no dogma; nothing artificial or doctrinaire, no hidden motives or post-war aims kept discreetly secret. As for the English scattered among them, they trusted us. They knew that what we and they were up to was the same. If we ever let them down, they blamed the hard circumstances of war and, better still, forgave all our mistakes. It made people rub their eyes in amazement that this proverbial home of individuality, lawlessness and revolt should unite, when the need came, in this durable harmony; but so it was.

All this, and wondering what the next phase would be, overcast leaving time. But it was another side of the Cretans of which there has been no room at all in this narrative which one knew one would miss most: the flair for friendship, company, talk, fun and music; originality and inventiveness in conversation and an explosive vitality that seems to recharge itself from the high voltage of the air; it was to the air, too, that they gave the credit for their capacity to cross several mountain ranges at the same lightning speed on an empty stomach as after swallowing enough raki and wine to lame other mortals for a week. Their glance and their speech were equally unguarded; there was something both patrician and bohemian in their attitude to life and their sense of the comic drew a thread of humour through everything – not frivolously, out of stoicism rather, if things were going badly – and to wipe away anything maudlin or rhetorical from matters that were too serious to be blurred by either. Recalcitrant to official dragooning, they would let themselves be cut to bits for the abstract ideas round which their lives turned. In a way, of course, they were ready for all that was happening. They were brought up on powder and shot and on traditions of fighting against occupation; they knew all about the cost of a wedding feast. Even if the whole place went up in smoke, they knew they would win in the end; if not this time, then the next. When eating and drinking in sheepfolds and caves it was to take anything stagey out of the utterances that they adopted a mock-heroic and almost ribald tone when they clashed glasses together and said, '*Let us die without shame!*'; but they meant it, and did.

★

But in the end excitement at the thought of getting the General off the island and being free at last from the disaster of failure (and, less creditably, from the *bruta figura*) had us all in its grip. Anyway, this time, the whole party, except for Grigori and Antoni Zoidakis, were coming too; for it was them I had been thinking about and would miss most. They'd been utterly beyond praise, and – of all the participators, before and after the capture, who had passed us on from hand to hand like an explosive and incendiary baton in two relay races across a dozen mountain ranges lasting for twenty-two and then seventeen days – their help had been instantaneous, enthusiastic and total with never a flicker of hesitation or doubt.

Manoli, Andrea, Kotsiphis and I climbed down from the rocks and the roots in the afternoon to see what the Germans were up to. All was quiet. Andrea went up the cliff again and we lay and smoked behind a rock until the others should come. Manoli reckoned we must have seen about four hundred people since the capture. Knowing Crete, he went on with a wry smile, many hundreds more must have a pretty good idea of our whereabouts by now; yet here we were.

To avoid the look of too large a procession the others came down in two parties and we all lay up till nightfall on a ledge in a deep hollow of the cliffs where an icy spring trickled down the rocks. An old Rodakiniot had walled it in with sea boulders to make a little grotto like a hermitage, deeply shaded by fig trees and oleanders. We soaked Stathi's hard bread and munched it with the old man's onions and lettuces and radishes and sat talking until long after dark. Then we crossed the short distance to the little cove we hoped to leave from. It seemed to us all, with its walls of rock on either side and the sand and the pebbles, the lapping of the water and the stars, a quiet place for our adventure to end.

As we stood about, talking in whispers at first, though there was no one to be afraid of, Andartes climbed down the rocks in two and threes to join us. There were the Rodakino Kapitans Khombitis and Manoli Yanna and Andrea Kotsiphis, and there too, suddenly, with the great fair moustache that had made us christen him Beowulf, was Petraka,* the Kapitan of the Asi Gonia band and one of our oldest friends on the island. He had brought a contingent of Goniots to join the other Andartes in guarding our departure and also to say goodbye.

The place was filling up like a drawing room: groups were lounging about in the rocks or strolling with slung guns quietly conversing; somewhere, led here for evacuation and discreetly tucked away at the back to avoid embarrassing the General, were the two Germans taken prisoner in the fight in Rodakino. Somewhere, too, the Five Times Lovely One must have been lurking. Quietly composed, with his sling neatly retied by Manoli, the General sat on a rock by the water's edge. I said it would be nice for him to be in a bunk with sheets after all our ups and downs. Billy told him we would all soon be eating lobster sand-wiches – the Captain of the ship was famous for them. The General smiled – 'Danke, Herr Major. Merci, mon Capitaine' – as much at the intention as the prospect of these delights. He had had a rotten time, and he knew we were trying to be nice.

Signalling was to begin at 10 o'clock – (not Monkey King after all, but S.B. – Sugar Baker) once every five minutes. To our consternation we realised that neither of us knew what B was in Morse code; only S from SOS. Billy flashed the three short dots, then a sort of 'S' something, in the hopes that Brian Coleman, the Captain, would make allowances for our not being regular soldiers.

At last we all thought we could hear the ship's engine and a wave of excitement ran along the beach. Then, after a series of faster signals, the sound grew fainter and seemed to die away and a mood of dismay assailed us all. These awful moments often occurred on beaches at times like these. Perhaps it was because

* Petraka had had a remarkable career. He had been a guerrilla in Macedonia fighting against the Turks and the Bulgarian Comitadais before the Balkan wars; he had also been Venizelos's bodyguard. A few months after the time we are dealing with, he was shot clean through the chest, in one side and out the other, in a fight with the Germans; but by some extraordinary fluke the bullet touched nothing vital.

one's ears, after straining out to sea, played tricks; but today there was a real reason for concern.

This agony was suddenly resolved by the arrival of Dennis, who was also due to leave. Fortunately, he knew the Morse code and we started desperately flashing with the correct signal; and at last, faint at first, then gradually louder, the sound of the ship came to us and a great sigh of relief rose from the waterline. (It occurs to me now that we ought to have asked the General. He must have been as eager to go now as we were. Did we not think of it, or was it shame at our amateur status?)

There was a slight coil of mist over the sea so it was not till she was quite close that we saw the ship. We could hear the rattle of the anchor going down; then two boats were lowered; they headed for the shore full of dark shapes. We had forgotten all about George Jellicoe's raiding forces. We could soon see that the boats were manned by figures in berets and jerkins all bristling with sub-machine guns. When the keels touched the pebbles, they leapt into the shallow water and rushed ashore full tilt; I heard someone shout my name. They thought we might have had to retreat, fighting to the rendezvous. When they saw that we were unsoiled, I think they were all a bit downcast, especially the Commander, who was not Jellicoe, but Bob Bury, whom I hadn't seen for three years. I introduced him to all the party and to the guerrilla leaders who were crowding about us in a state of great jubilation, and to the General. He bowed stiffly, shook hands and said: '*Sehr gefällig, Herr General*,' in a perfect accent.

The moment had come. Bob Bury and his commandos emptied their rucksacks of all their stores and cigarettes and handed them over to those of our companions who were remaining. We all pulled off our boots to leave behind; this was always done; even in rags they came in useful. Soon we were saying goodbye to Petraka and the Rodakino Kapitans and Yanni Katsias and the guerrillas and lastly to Antoni Zoidakis. We all embraced like grizzly bears. I tried to persuade Antoni to come with us; he wavered a moment and then decided against it. I wish he had. A sailor said, '*Excuse me, sir, but we ought to get a move on.*'

As we neared the ship, the figures waving along the shore had begun to grow indistinct among the shadows and, very fast, it was hard to single out the cove from the tremendous mountain mass that soared from the sea to the Milky Way. The ship grew larger, her pom-poms and Bofors anti-aircraft guns shining in the starlight. When we drew alongside sailors in spotless white were reaching down into the bulwarks to guide the General up the rope ladder ('*That's right, sir! Easy does it!*') while we – Billy, Manoli and George and I – helped from below. A moment later we were on the deck in our bare feet and it was all over.

WAR REPORTS

Crete, 1942–1945

Introduction

During his time as a British Army officer concerned with covert operations in Crete, Patrick Leigh Fermor wrote nine reports about his activities. All were written for the headquarters of the Special Operations Executive, the British organisation charged with encouraging resistance and carrying out sabotage in enemy-occupied territory. Original typed copies survive among Leigh Fermor's personal papers, which are preserved today as a collection in his name in the archives of the National Library of Scotland.

The nine reports vary greatly in length, content and tone. Often they were rushed affairs, penned on the move and against the clock after news arrived of an imminent sortie to the coast by the Royal Navy. When it came to staying in touch with the outside world, a secret rendezvous with the Navy, when men and stores were perhaps being deposited on the shore and evacuees picked up, was a rare and precious event. Ordinarily, British officers on Crete kept in contact with SOE headquarters by clandestine wireless transmitters. SOE-trained operators, Greek and British, were responsible for handling these sets and maintaining that vital link, which was used to dispatch short reports, receive instructions, and call in supplies by air and sea. But it was a time-consuming job and messages were necessarily concise. The chance to send a written account out of the country, through the hands of the Royal Navy, offered an opportunity to say and explain much more.

Several themes are common to most of Leigh Fermor's reports, such as Cretan morale, German morale, working conditions and plans. One consequence of the haste in which he wrote them is their rather irregular structure. Leigh Fermor was a trained and experienced intelligence officer, yet several reports, though they begin with neat passages under standard military headings ('Enemy Morale' 'Propaganda'), rapidly descend into rushed summaries, heavy with anecdote, of recent doings and personal experiences. The striking informality with which they are written is explained by the fact that he knew his likely audience: namely, officers of the Cretan desk at SOE headquarters in Cairo, including colleagues who had themselves worked clandestinely on Crete.

The passages that follow represent about a third of Leigh Fermor's original text. Ranging from colourful descriptions of conditions in which he was living and characters he was meeting, to accounts of daring forays, in disguise, into German-held towns, they have been selected for inclusion on the grounds that they illuminate his personal experiences on the island. They also include passages that underline the less romantic realities of behind-the-lines warfare: Leigh Fermor's involvement in the execution of traitors, for example, and the terrible and tragic death of his friend, Yanni Tsangarakis.

Long lists of German dispositions, together with complex accounts of local politics and guerrilla machinations, comprise much of what has been omitted. Readers interested in those aspects of Leigh Fermor's work can consult, by appointment, the original copies of his reports that are now held in Edinburgh, or read the less complete versions that survive at the National Archives in Kew, outside London, where, among SOE's surviving files, reports by many of his colleagues can also be found.

Glossary of Pseudonyms

Like all British officers working secretly on Crete, Leigh Fermor was wary of the danger of his reports falling into the wrong hands. For that reason, he made heavy and frequent use of colourful pseudonyms in order to disguise the names and identities of locations, local helpers and compatriots. In the extracts that follow, each pseudonym is explained at the first mention for the purposes of clarity. For ease of reference, they are also listed below.

PERSONS

ALEC T.	Alec Tarves, SOE wireless operator
ARTHUR	Arthur Reade, SOE officer
BARNES	Captain Dick Barnes, SOE officer
BEOWULF	Petros Papadopetrakis
BINGO	Corporal Bingham, SOE wireless operator
BO-PEEP	Kapetan Manoli Bandouvas, guerrilla leader
CH[ARIDIMOS]	SANCHO's nephew, in Egypt
CHANGEBUG	Georgis Psychoundakis
CHIMP	Lieutenant Nikolaos Lampethakes, SOE officer
DOC	Dr Ioannes Paizes
EMMANUEL THE COPPER	Manoli Paterakis
FISHY	Lieutenant Elevtherios Psaroudakes
GRIGORI	Grigorios Khnaras

HARRY	Staff Sergeant Harry Brooke, SOE wireless operator
HERCULES	Assistant to MI6 officer Ralph Stockbridge
HIPPO	Hippokrates Antonakes
JEHU	Antonios Katsias
JELLICOE	George Jellicoe, SBS officer
JOHN	John Stanley, Inter-Services Liaison Department
KANAKI	Yanni Tsangarakis's brother
LEONIDAS	Another Cretan helper
LOPEZ	Emmanuel Paradeisianos
MANOLI THE MINOTAUR CALF	Emmanuel Ntibirakes
MATT	Matthew White, SOE wireless operator
MAURICE	Lieutenant Colonel Nikolaos Plevres
MINOAN MIKE	Michael Akoumianakis
MOKE	Elevtherios Kourakes
NIKO	Lieutenant Nikolaos Soures, SOE officer
NIMROD	Demetrios Vassilakes
ORESTES	Pericles Vandoulakes
PLOUSIOS	Vangeli Vandoulakes
PLOUSIOS family	Vandoulakes family
PTOCHOS	Apostolos Evangelou, PLF's one-time wireless operator
PYLADES	Ioannes Androulakes
RALPH	Ralph Stockbridge
SANCHO	Yanni Tsangarakis, PLF's guide and friend
SELFRIDGE	Kapetan Petrakogeorgis
STIFF	Ioannes Dramountanes
TWEEDLEDEE	Kostas Kastrinogiannes
TWEEDLEDUM	Aristeides Kastrinogiannes

VICAR	Father Ioannes Alevizakis
YANNAKO M. (39)	Ioannes Manouras

Places

BABYLON	Heraklion
BADLANDS	Messara plain
BATTISTA	Agios Ioannes
BEEHIVE	Hideout above Gournes; Canea HQ
BOSOMS	Vyzari
CAMELOT	Anogia
CASTLES	Kastelli Pediados
CORNERS	Gonies
EOTHEN	Seteia
FLAILS	Alones village (Rethymno)
KATZPHUR	Phourphoura
LOTUSLAND	Amari valley
MOUNTAINS of MORNE	Asterousia mountains
NINEVEH	Rethymno
OUTRIVER	Unidentified location
ST HELENS	Agios Konstantinos (Rethymno)
SNOWDON	Mount Ida
SODOM	Vianno plateau
STARLIGHT	Photeinou (Rethymno)
STUBBORN CORNER	Asi Gonia (Sphakia)
TREASURETOWN	Argyroupolis (Rethymno)
TROJAN GATE	Canea Gate
TROY	Canea/Chania
TUSCAN mountains	Lasithi mountains
TUSCANY	Lasithi
UPPER JOSEPH	Apano Siphi
VILLENEUVE	Neapolis
ZINC	Unidentified south coast location

Report No. 1

June 1942 to February 1943

Patrick Leigh Fermor was put ashore on the south coast of Axis-occupied Crete on 23 June 1942. A combined force of Italian and German troops, many thousands strong, was holding the island at that time, and his instructions were in line with those of other British officers at large on the island: work with Cretans hostile to the occupation; gather intelligence; and seek to undermine enemy spirits and strength by sabotage and subversion. From August 1942 until early 1943 he had charge of the western half of the island and the mountainous provinces (routinely described in his reports as 'nomes') of Chania and Rethymno ('Retimo' as he spelled it).

Almost eight months after landing on the island, Leigh Fermor managed to dispatch his first written report. He began writing it in early January 1943 and finished it in mid-February. A good deal of his text was devoted to cataloguing enemy troop dispositions, numbers, coastal defences and communications. He allowed himself freer rein when discussing Axis and Cretan morale, guerrilla politics and politicking, German counter-espionage activities, and his own plans, subversive activities and day-to-day experiences. The latter included an uncomfortable period spent evading German patrols; it was not yet over when he wrote what follows.

~

5 January 1943

. . . This report is being compiled in uncomfortable circumstances and under difficulties, as my new area is suffering from an acute attack of Hun-trouble that keeps my HQ pretty well on the run . . .

ENEMY TROOPS

Although the rôle of CRETE is now purely defensive, enemy troops in the two provinces have not increased in numbers on as large a scale as I expected. It is hard to keep an exact check on numbers – in towns and transit camps it is almost impossible – but one can form a general idea of the total from collecting the most reliable military opinions at one's disposal, and finding the average. The numbers supplied always vary. It is, I think, pretty near the truth to say that Hun troops in CANEA province amount to about 30,000, and in RETIMO province, about 8,000 . . .

Little provision is made by the enemy for troop movements across rocky or mountainous country, as they rightly consider that they make on the whole very rough going for regular troops, unaided by former reconnaissance, and preclude the advance of troops in any but the most ragged formation. This is where the co-operation of Cretan irregular bands with our troops will prove so invaluable [in the event of an Allied invasion] . . .

The [German] GOC [General Officer Commanding] CRETE, in a recent order to the Crete Garrison, said: 'We will, in the event of an invasion, defend Crete to the last man and the last round', and there is no doubt that they do not intend to relinquish the island, the capture of which is one of their outstanding triumphs, and one that cost them dear, without a hard fight. They are frightened of an invasion, and the senior officers are frightened of two other factors because they are imponderables: morale in the rank and file, and Cretan action in the event of a landing . . .

GERMAN MORALE

When I landed in CRETE nearly eight months ago, the first bit of information I learnt was that the same day the [enemy garrison in] TIMBAKI . . . had made a victory march through the town under the eyes of a despondent crowd, in celebration of the capture of TOBRUK. I assumed that their AFRICAN triumphs would have filled them with high spirits, but (paradoxically, I thought) every report of German conversation with Cretans told the same tale of depression and disgust at the possibility of being sent to the desert. Cretans said that soldiers leaving for AFRICA burst into tears and declared that they would never come back alive, but Cretans will say anything. Throughout the EL ALAMEIN stalemate, stories of depression and war weariness kept coming in, and tales of odd Huns buying civilian clothes, and begging Cretans to hide them till the English could take them prisoner, in the event of a landing. I took all this with a huge pinch of salt.

When the news of our break-through came, then of our advance into CYRENAICA, tales circulated of German soldiers attacking HITLER ('Scheiss HITLER' is the favourite phrase), of bad discipline, failure to salute officers, and of drunkenness. Since then, things have gone steadily downhill. No doubt much of this is Cretan embroidery, but the Germans do seem to be thoroughly war weary and no longer believe that they will win it. The Russian victories, the fall of TRIPOLI and STALINGRAD in the same fortnight and the bombing of BERLIN, have all borne their fruit.

Two months ago, I spent a long evening in ST HELENS [the village of Agios Konstantinos] . . . in the next room to that of two German sergeants, listening in. They were depressed and fed up, above all at spending the fourth Christmas 'weit von der Heimat' [far from home]. They sang a few songs about the Rhineland, and heaved great sighs. Then, to my astonishment, they started an English lesson. I felt like correcting their pronunciation through the door. When they went out to dinner I went into their room with a petrol lighter and hunted around. (I pinched the manual of a German W/T set, which may or may not be interesting.) I dropped the lighter and had a feverish hunt on all fours for it and the door, and got back to my room just before they came back, slightly drunk. The lesson went on, they had a discussion about England. One was frankly pro-English; the other slightly so. The conversation petered out almost in tears about this war with their 'first cousins'. We were all in bed by now, and their final words were that the war should end soon, without much worry as to which side won . . .

I think it may be fairly stated that German morale in Crete at the moment is at a very low ebb. Just to what extent it may militate in our favour when the time comes is problematical, but it is quite certain that the soldiers now here will not fight with the same conviction as they would have a year ago. They are growing daily more uneasy about their past treatment of the Cretans, and readjust their approach accordingly in an effort to mollify them. As this is going on at the same time as redoubled forced labour, requisitioning (German 'Q' side seems to be almost non-existent as far as food is concerned), cattle theft, raids, arrests and beatings-up, it doesn't cut much ice. They know the Cretans hate them and are living for the moment to dig up their rifles and say it with bullets . . .

The growing fear of a Cretan 'stab in the back' is well illustrated by the various orders published in Greek from [German] GHQ [General Headquarters] Crete. At first they were threatening and ruthless in tone. The most recent TON KRETIKON LAON (which I am appending to this report) is significant for several reasons. Firstly, the tone is conciliatory, almost wheedling. Secondly, it shows that high German authorities fear an imminent invasion, and are eager, at the eleventh hour, to cajole the Cretans into non-combatancy. Paragraph two runs: 'All we desire is that the Cretans should think as Cretans, and that their *own* interests should outweigh all else, for the good of their country. In other words, every right-thinking Cretan should remain outside this struggle, both the overt and the covert struggle.' The defensive note in para. 3 is worth noting: 'We are strong enough to wage and win this war against the English.' More bum sucking in para. 3: 'So

every Cretan who thinks as a genuine Cretan will behave honour-
ably, will remain a spectator, and will obey orders that are essential to law and order.' Para. 3 continues further down with the
statement: 'Agents, spies and saboteurs have greatly multiplied in
numbers recently' (!) 'Real Cretans must offer no refuge or support
to saboteurs and leaders or guerrilla bands' (!) 'It is your duty to
track down and repel every enemy attack, all enemy propaganda,
all enemy activities of such men, whose only wish is to bring
trouble and war once more into your country' – 'Little Crete' as
it is called lower down. The document winds up into another
exhortation to think as Cretans and of Cretan interests.

The parts about Agents, spies, saboteurs and irregulars is
revealing, and clearly the result of a bad nervous state and scraps
of information about our activities, badly pieced together. The
Germans are frightened of the mountains, and though they never
actually *see* the blood-thirsty guerrillas (which is scarcely strange,
as except for SELFRIDGE [Kapetan Petrakogeorgis] and BO-PEEP
[the guerrilla leader Manoli Bandouvas] there are none!) they
imagine that a horde of them hides behind each rock just out of
sight. Every bush an ambush.

It is interesting to learn that XAN [Fielding] and ARTHUR
[Reade]'s joining TOM [Dunbabin] and me is considered a great
increase in numbers! Perhaps this is what a skeleton army means.

A friend of mine in a mountain village had a [German] Lieutenant
billeted on him for the night. When he opened the bedroom
door in the morning to take in his washing water, there was a
clatter of chairs and tin trays and mugs which had been propped
against the door as a primitive burglar alarm. The Lieutenant was
sitting bolt upright in bed clutching his sub-machine gun, his eyes
popping out of his head.

Propaganda . . .

The above facts being as they are, and the German mind being
so open to auto-suggestion of a disturbing nature, it is a pity that

more use has not been made of [propaganda leaflets dropped by the RAF] . . . [T]he only trouble incurred would seem to be that of compiling the right kind of stuff, printing it *en masse*, and getting it delivered to the [air force] formations briefed for Cretan [air] raids in time, who would drop the leaflets as a matter of course . . . This kind of warfare was no doubt futile at the outset of the war, but, in Crete at any rate, this easy form of activity would repay many times over the small trouble incurred, in helping to undermine an already unsatisfactory morale . . .

The reading matter should be bogey-bogey, and make their flesh creep (SERIOUS WARNING! IF, WHEN YOU ARE OUR PRISONERS (which you soon will be) you expect us to save you from the fury of the Cretan population, etc. etc. etc.) OR the phoney-friendly type: 'Aren't you getting tired, German soldier? What are you heading for? Last year you hoped to take MOSCOW, LENINGRAD and ALEXANDRIA. You have just lost STALINGRAD, TOBRUK, BENGHAZI, TRIPOLI. What about *tomorrow*? *And next year?*' Play on their homesickness and sentimentality . . .

If morale of troops has any influence on battles, this is important, as I am convinced that such a campaign would do a lot, now that we have solid facts to back our claims, to accelerate morale deterioration . . .

Two months ago I laid on a campaign, cooperating with TOM, for scrawling defeatist and communist slogans wherever they might catch German eyes – on barrack walls, signposts, in latrines, etc., necessarily short, as Greek personnel had to be trained in writing Latin characters, and mistakes would have defeated the purpose of the scheme, which was to give the impression that Hun soldiers had written them, that the [German] army was in a state of covert mutiny, defeatism and political unorthodoxy, in the hopes that they might follow the lead. They were: 'Heil Stalin!' 'Heil Moskau!' (accompanied by the hammer and sickle). 'We want to go home' 'Down with Hitler!' 'Where is our Air Force?' 'The Führer is a swine!' and suchlike simple stuff. In some regions it went off at half-cock, in others well, and may have done some good. It is worth using later on. I always write up elaborate slogans in bold gothic type when I get a suitable place, and nobody watching . . .

GERMAN SECURITY MEASURES, COUNTER-ESPIONAGE, ETC.

Now that the island has an exclusively defensive rôle, the enemy have woken up to the fact that British agents are at work in CRETE, that information is being sent out, and that there exist Cretan bodies in an organised or semi-organised state, and they are paying much attention to these matters, and are far more efficient . . . For the ferreting out of hostile activity they rely on: –

GERMANOPHILES AND TRAITORS

. . . who also supply them with any information they can, which is now not much, as most of them are known by the rest of the Cretans, who keep away from them. Also they are becoming afraid for their lives, now that the tide of war has turned . . .

AGENTS PROVOCATEURS

. . . These are a far more dangerous weapon, and they operate in different ways, that may be roughly divided into three: –

a) *Germans masquerading* as escaped British prisoners, pseudo or real Cypriots in German pay, who wander from village to village to discover who are the people that feed and hide real escaped prisoners . . .

b) *The Black Marketeer*, and anyone with a pretext for wandering from place to place and contacting large numbers of people (e.g. the Russian Armenian (?) who sold Tommy-gun bullets, informed the enemy of the whereabouts of hidden arms, and encompassed the arrest of one of his customers).

c) *The false friend* . . . who professes sympathy with the cause, worms his way into confidence, extracts and sends back information, transmits false information, and finally, when he has exploited his territory to the utmost, informs the enemy that his source has run dry, and that they can now take military action on his information. This is by far the most dangerous type, and I am sure, the instigator of the present round-up.

MILITARY ACTION

a) *Arms Searches.* The size of the [German] unit detailed is fifty and upwards. They usually arrive by day (so that arms cannot be smuggled out in the dark) with only comparative surprise value. Information is often obtained beforehand by our friends, so that a general clean-up may be staged. The population is herded into the Church or school, and the search takes place with much incidental looting . . . The number of arms found is usually small, and mostly sporting guns. The owners are arrested and imprisoned but I have not heard of recent cases of people being shot for this.

b) *Surrounding a Village.* In hopes of Big Game more trouble to secure surprise is taken over this. Troops from 200 to 500 approach the village by night and remain in position till dawn. All access and egress is barred, and the search continues as in (a) except that all is stricter. Floors and gardens are dug up, prisoners taken, flogged and threatened on the spot, or offered bribes and security in Germany if they will talk . . .

PRISON METHODS

Every means is used [by the Germans] on prisoners to extract information; solitary confinement in small cells; starvation; threats of torture; severe flogging with rods or leather covered sticks or strips; bright lights, etc. There have been several cases of prisoners being shot in secret (e.g. . . . PTOCHOS [Apostolos Evangelou, Leigh Fermor's one-time wireless operator]). This is owing to German unwillingness to broadcast the presence of enemy espionage in CRETE.

If the Germans have failed in their primary aim of rounding up all agents and organisers, they have several times succeeded in their secondary aim of creating conditions that make work impossible. By keeping us on the run, and helped by obvious treachery, driving our main collaborators into the hills . . .

How Can Crete Cooperate with a British Landing?

. . . The reaction of the average Cretan, on hearing that the British have landed at last, will be to dig his rifle out of his vineyard, fill his pockets with rounds, stick a knife in his belt, and set out for the nearest Germans with his friends and start shooting them. And very nice too. Those without arms will try to steal or capture them. But, comparatively well armed as Crete is, there are not enough arms to go around, and many of them are rusted and useless through long hiding. This does not obtain in the neighbourhood of the SPHAKIA road, where the villages are stiff with loot from the British retreat in 1941. So all that follows presupposes the dropping of arms immediately preceding operations. Ammunition (.303 and Mannlicher) is also urgently needed, but not, in general, till the last minute. The other weapon most in demand is the hand grenade, a favourite arm with Cretans, and very suitable for the rocky country.

A few days – perhaps hours – before operations begin, the

Cretans could do useful work by shooting up outlying villages, and declaring an insurrection. This would draw troops into the interior and shake the Germans' nerves to an important extent. Other bodies, properly organised, could attack key points in the rear and flank to direct the enemy fire and give our troops an opportunity to land and deploy unhindered. Others could wipe out posts simultaneously. The parties detailed to attack communications could cut telephone wires, spread broken glass on the roads, shoot up traffic, and others, attack, if not wipe out, certain larger enemy garrisons and prevent them leaving their base for the scene of action . . .

Most Cretans expect a landing soon, in spite of our evasive 'go slow' counsel. They are living for the moment to take up arms, and can be relied upon to give a good account of themselves. There will be a lot of prisoner shooting, a certain amount of atrocities and a great deal of wiping out of old scores.

WANDERING ENGLISH ESCAPEES ETC.

As far as I can make out, there are forty to sixty of these in RETIMO and CANEA. Many of them are installed in families, but others lead a wretched life from village to village, being fed by a population that is terrified of German reprisals. Things have grown easier since our change of fortune in the desert, and on the whole the winter has been more merciful than anyone expected from the point of view of food and weather. There is a small minority that never wanted to return to EGYPT, and now there are many who feel that they would like to see the end of German rule in CRETE now they have waited so long. One or two cause alarm in the villages that support them by getting blind drunk and rolling down the street singing 'Ilkley Moor' and 'A Troopship was leaving Bombay' at the top of their voices. Generally speaking, their position is better than it was four months ago. I give those I see cash and cigarettes as frequently as possible . . .

Transport

Transport by donkey is becoming very difficult, and of suspicious goods (W/T [wireless transmitter], charges, batteries, sweets and toys [explosives]) virtually impossible for long distances, owing, now, not so much to the scarcity of beasts as the plentifulness of Germans, who now penetrate into mountain regions formerly Hun-free. Gear, therefore, has to be lugged from point to point on one's back by remote mountain tracks, and it is no joke. In autumn no animals were available, as they were all being used for work in the fields. There was a great scarcity of messengers at the same time. Both these difficulties have improved (so the donkey was never bought!) but the German situation grows daily worse . . .

Food

. . . When I arrived the food situation was poor, though I cannot claim ever to have gone seriously hungry. In the Summer one ate beans, lentils, tomatoes, potatoes, cheese, bread (sometimes scarce), meat sometimes, and oil. Now there is nearly everything one could wish, washed down by plenty of wine and raki from a good vintage autumn . . .

My experience is that, though some of the food is impalatable [sic] to Englishmen at first (and some always), one grows fat and bouncing in CRETE . . .

Weather

It has been a singularly mild winter, by all accounts, although there has been plenty of snow in the mountains, and plenty of rain, especially in the late autumn. Today – the 10th February – is like Spring. The main trouble is the cold at night in the various caves and huts we inhabit.

Working Conditions

Work gets more difficult as the winter months go by . . .

At STARLIGHT [Photeinou, in Rethymno] we went through a bad patch – 15 Huns with guns coming up the slope to our cave, with PTOCHOS, back towards them, tapping away with earphones on, twenty yards away. SANCHO [Yanni Tsangarakis, Leigh Fermor's guide and friend] and I dared not move (we were in the lying load position, ready to sell ourselves dearly, in the finest tradition). The Huns walked straight past, up the hill. It was wonderful. We packed up quick and beat it.

Then – at the end of October – I started up my two stations, one in CANEA Nome with PTOCHOS operating, the other in RETIMO with Sgt. JOE BRADLEY [another SOE wireless operator]. Then both the sets went wrong, but were finally put right, and everything was going swimmingly at last. I was starting to get to know all the big boys and to work up an information service in RETIMO . . . Everything looked splendid and I felt I was getting somewhere (It takes anyone at least two months to get into the feel of an area in this job, and make the necessary contacts) . . . [Then a spate of local] arrests took place, and put my CANEA station out of action . . . All the PLOUSIOS [Vandoulakes] family took to the hills, PLOUSIOS himself [Vangeli Vandoulakes] became automatically not much use, being hunted, and ORESTES [Pericles Vandoulakes] in a fair way to getting shot. So that was that, and I thanked heaven we had the RETIMO station, and BRADLEY. Life was very interesting. I started wandering about without guides (who always stop you going anywhere near Germans) and seeing as much of the Huns as I could, listening in to their conversations etc . . .

Meanwhile I was having my new CANEA HQ laid on in a shepherd's hut high up in the White Mountains . . . [After Christmas and] on the way back to FLAILS [the village of Alones in Rethymno], [I] learnt that 2–300 Huns had raided it that night, taken numerous prisoners including SIPHI, the VICAR [Father Ioannes Alevizakis]'s son with 2 letters of mine in his pocket, saying nothing fortunately to his father. SANCHO, who was sleeping in the village, managed to slip through the cordon and up to the set, where he woke up both operators, hid the stuff and stayed on guard while they beat it into the hills. It was a great feat . . . We went to STUBBORN CORNER [Asi Gonia in Sphakia], where . . . BEOWULF [Petros Papadopetrakis] . . . hid us all in a cave – the whole district was stiff with Huns, who thought they were close on the scent at last – and ALEC T[arves, another SOE wireless operator] and I with some Corner-boys set off over the hills to the mountains above FLAILS – and lugged all our gear along the ridge to our cave. Meanwhile grim tales were coming in of the goings on at FLAILS, arrests, beatings up etc. A friend saw SIPHI the VICAR's son being taken through TREASURETOWN [Argyroupolis in Rethymno] with blood streaming out of his mouth. The VICAR and his brother the Mayor escaped into the hills. The Germans went back every day to try and discover more; they knew the set had been there, and had found an old battery . . . Their interrogations of prisoners showed they had all details about me (appearance, dress etc) and SANCHO, who was already being hunted.

Towards the end of January I moved over to my [new] CANEA HQ with XAN and ALEC T. sending BRADLEY back to TOM's in order to catch the next boat. I was very sorry to see him go, as he had worked splendidly under trying circumstances and been a cheerful and amusing companion. His quickly learnt Greek made him friends everywhere. At the BEEHIVE (CANEA HQ) [a hideout above Gournes] we found ARTHUR [Reade] had shifted house about a mile, as he had become widely known, and, with his now long red beard, had become a popular figure in the neighbourhood; pilgrims came from miles around to visit the English General. His high spirits and charm kept my Canea area in a state of high morale and interest during my RETIMO absence. The day after ALEC T. and I arrived (XAN had gone down with a bad foot in the plain), 3 German columns of sixty each came up either side of our valley, closing the mouth of it. We hid the stuff, and climbed up one side of it, and finally into an umbrageous cypress tree, whence we watched them beating around for our hide-out; fortunately they were misled by their impressed guide, a friend of ours, and came streaming down again, all their disappointed comments, and grumbling at the rock climbing being music to us. One of our guides, MOKE [Elevtherios Kourakes], got two bullets in the leg breaking through the cordon, and COSTI, his cousin, only got through by opening up with his revolver. The CHANGEBUG [Georgios Psychoundakis] did not reappear – it was snowing hard now – and after a day I took out a search party, without result. He turned up later having made a long circuit to warn XAN in the plains.

We had to shift the set again, as our tracks in the snow were an easy guide to anyone after us. On the fourth of February I sent SANCHO and ALEC up into the wilds to get contact with you, which at last he managed to do. XAN had arrived now, and he, ARTHUR and I took up quarters in an underground grotto. The Germans began thrashing round the country again after 'British officers', came fairly near, and went away again. Then the news arrived of the impending arrival of the boat, and I had to get SANCHO down quick, hand over to XAN, and make for HERAKLION nome – no mean distance from the heart of CANEA; writing up this report in great haste and at odd moments on the way . . . in caves and huts . . . So any disorderliness or odd sequence of headings will be excused, I hope. I am now in an elfin grotto in the MESSARA, TOM sleeping beside me, and my nominees for evacuation – the VICAR, DOC [Dr Ioannes Paizes], ORESTES, PLOUSIOS and the CHANGEBUG (whom the Huns have been after for three months) – huddled round the walls in different attitudes of dejection. We were all soaked through last night in a hellish march through the dark. Odds and ends of BO-PEEP's and SELFRIDGE's gangs are fondling their guns . . . It is very much the same atmosphere as when I arrived. It is my twenty-eighth birthday.

Report No. 2

February to April 1943

Leigh Fermor's second report was written two and a half months after his first. By then he had a new role. When Tom Dunbabin, the senior SOE officer on the island, left for Cairo in mid-February 1943, Leigh Fermor took over his work in and around the capital, Heraklion ('Babylon' in his reports). It was a job that required him to move out of the mountains, base himself closer to the coast and engage in work of a more political and intelligence-gathering nature.

Much of Leigh Fermor's second report was devoted, as before, to detailing enemy positions, morale and strength, the politics and activities of Cretan guerrilla bands and political movements, and his own efforts at organising anti-Axis sabotage and subversion. As the following extracts show, his new appointment allowed him to operate in Heraklion in disguise and look more closely at the possibilities of sabotaging enemy shipping ('fish') with explosives ('sweets' and 'toys') in the harbour ('the fishpond').

~

27 April 1943

. . . AXIS MORALE

German morale is very much the same as described at some length in my last report, but more so. Bombing in Germany[,] the Russian stalemate and their desert reverses, are all telling, though the action of all these factors is delayed by the reticence and mendaciousness of the Hun propaganda system . . .

They are making an eleventh hour bid for popularity [with the Cretans] which, though vain on the whole, is less clumsy than their usual psychological manoeuvrings. I think the amnesty was a *bona fide* effort to court Cretan good-will, rather than bait to attract the anti-German elements, with the purpose of getting their measure for later arrest, though this was no doubt a secondary motive. They know what they have to fear from the Cretans, and are now bitterly lamenting their former harshness. Their line of approach is now 'We are all brothers united against the threat of bolshevism, and we must work hand-in-hand'. Knowing Cretan sympathies, they have wisely eased up on anti-British propaganda, and selections from CHURCHILL's past attacks on Soviet RUSSIA are printed in Cretan newspapers as slogans. There is a great anti-communist drive in progress . . .

In general, German manners have shown a marked change for the better, which is highly undesirable, as German brutality and bloodiness are one of our best allies . . .

Little need be said of the Italians. They are war weary and defeatist to an extreme degree. In Babylon [Heraklion], I heard a young Italian friend of Yanni A[ndroulakes]'s, say to the latter: – 'Don't you think because we didn't fight in Albania, that Italians can't fight. You wait and see how we fight the Germans!' Later on, over his wine, he said 'Viva Ingliterra!' with great gusto. Italian nonsense, of course, but indication of a trend. Hostile incidents between Huns and Italians are too frequent to record. Last month an Italian threw a hand grenade at 3 Huns in the street, killed one and wounded two. The German authorities complained, and he was put through an Italian Court Martial and imprisoned. He was out and about in a fortnight.

CRETAN MORALE . . .

Excellent. They had a relapse in March – the Spring had come, the African campaign was still in progress, and an Allied landing in CRETE seemed no nearer. There was a growing feeling that CRETE would never be attacked, that the Allies would attack in Thrace, in Sicily, in France — anywhere but there, and that their servitude would drag ingloriously on till the end of the war. In my area, I assured them that this was nonsense, and said, with some solemnity, that there was absolutely no doubt that CRETE would be attacked and set free, but that I had no idea when this would be, and certainly not in the immediate future, and this has had a satisfactory effect. At the moment, morale is high everywhere, as a direct result of the Tunisian campaign . . .

PROPAGANDA

The [anti-German] pamphlets and posters [that Cairo had recently sent to Crete] were just what was needed, and I want lots more of them. I had a petrol tin made with the papers soldered into a false bottom, filled it with petrol, and sent it in to Babylon by car . . . George and PYLADES [Ioannes Androulakes] got busy the night I left Babylon, and stuck three . . . on the door of every single house where Huns are billeted, in lavatories, inside the passages of houses; on the Gestapo building door, and outside the Kreiskommandatur on all floors, outside mess rooms — in fact everywhere where the Huns could see them . . . It was a very thorough job. The result next morning was that all the Feldgendarmerie, Geheime Feldpolizei, Gestapo, Greek police, secret police and . . . stooges were set to work unsticking them, and as they were very numerous and firmly glued, they took some time to peel off, with interested crowds watching and being moved on, or cursed at by Huns scarlet in the face. Very many were collected by Hun soldiers and civilians and displayed to a wide circle. Nobody talked of anything else for days, and it had as useful effect among the Greeks as among the Huns. There is no doubt that it got right under the skin of the latter. A rigorous inspection of all parcels from Germany has been laid on, and many recent Hun arrivals from the mainland with chequered reports were arrested and examined. Billets of suspected Hun communities were ransacked, and a free fight started in one. 30 Huns were finally shot a week later, George informs me, *pour encourager les autres*, and hordes of plain clothes stooges dogged the footsteps of completely inoffensive private soldiers and citizens . . .

EVACUATIONS

. . . I would like to put forward the suggestion that W/T operators should be sent into CRETE for maximum periods of three months, unless they find the work particularly attractive, and wish to remain. Their life is an extremely dull one, and the only excitement they have is of the wrong sort – hiding from and running away from Huns. They suffer more than any of us from the lice, the rain, the cold, the lack of company, food and books . . .

FISHING WITH SWEETS AND TOYS

I do not want to discuss this in too much detail for obvious [security] reasons. But after a personal recce of the fish pool there seems to be a sporting chance of landing a couple of fish. Access can be gained by a rope ladder tied to a telegraph pole on a bastion above the pond. There is a difficult open stretch after this, with two Nasties on picket to be dodged, till the water is reached, and for this reason, a moonless night is essential. The operation is made more difficult because the fish we are after have recently adopted the habit of swimming to the northern end of the pool at night, which means a swim of two kilometres for us, half of it with the limpets. But it seems worth trying, and I intend to try it after Ralph [Stockbridge]'s arrival. The party consists of EMMANUEL the Copper [Manoli Paterakis], PYLADES, young GEORGE, and me.

Getting [the limpet mines] into Babylon was quite a saga – digging them out of the snow in the crevasse where they were hidden, lugging them down to the main road, and packing them (8), Sten gun, grenades and pistols in suitcases, when dusk fell. NIKO

[Lieutenant Nikolaos Soures, SOE officer], PYLADES, Copper MANOLI and I took them into BOSOMS [Vyzari], and stowed them on to the roof of JEHU [Antonios Katsias] of NINEVEH [Rethymno]'s bus. PYLADES and JEHU, both gripping revolvers, accompanied them to NINEVEH, JEHU driving, with several squareheads in the bus. At NINEVEH, JEHU's confrere NIMROD [Demetrios Vassilakes] of BABYLON was meant to be waiting with his bus to take them over. But it had been commandeered, so PYLADES parked them in sacks, put them on an ordinary bus, and drove to Babylon. When he unloaded them just inside the barbican, a Greek policeman walked up and said, 'Open those sacks, I want to see what's inside them!' PYLADES answered rudely, 'Mind your own business,' then, 'As a matter of fact, they are full of German tinned meat, and if we open them here, those Germans over there will pinch the lot. Have a couple, chum,' and he pulled two out of his pocket, hailing a cab at the same time. The policeman helped him pile them on, and he bowled off to his house, where he built them into the wall. It was very, very nice work . . .

Working Conditions and Personal Narrative

When the boat [that recently came to drop off personnel and stores] sailed away, our little party set off up the hill again, armed with rifles and bandoliers and ready for anything as I felt sure the neighbouring Germans *must* have heard the ship, the shouting and clatter, and seen the signals. CHIMP [Lieutenant Nikolaos Lampethakes, SOE officer] was not feeling fit, and we hid in a cave all night and all the next day, intending to push on at night again. We spent a lazy day, talking, smoking Players cigarettes (and what a delight it was), and waiting to see hordes of squareheads swarming along the shore below. But they didn't. We watched two of them out after hares up the hillside opposite with a terrier, utterly oblivious to anything unusual having happened the night before.

We moved off at moonrise, stopping to cook a meal in a deserted house in PLATANIES [6 kilometres from Treis Ekklesies].

There was not a sign of life anywhere, and all the prohibited area, awe inspiring at any time, seemed as remote and dead as the mountains in the moon. One shepherd (100% δικός μας) [100% ours] was the only human being anybody saw all the time we were in the zone . . .

We were all as heavily armed as pirates, and to stop people saying, 'A guerrilla band had passed' the next day, we adopted the device of pretending to be Huns when passing through villages. We made as much clatter and stamping as we could, each one of us shooting a set piece parrot wise at the top his voice: '*Sakrament noch einmal*' '*Herr Hauptmann! Herr Hauptmann!*' '*Komm, komm, Papier!*' '*Vino schnapps extra prima*', etc. The result was perfect. Doors were closed, windows hastily shuttered, and lingerers in the street dashed for their houses, terrified of being caught out after curfew, and we clanked through unobserved. Fortunately, we met no real Huns, which would have embarrassed everybody . . .

Working in this area, after my former haunts, is like settling down to a Jane Austen novel, after leaving a thriller by Sax Rohmer half way through. Merely the struggle for existence there is a full time job, though there are lulls. On looking back, my six months seem to have been one long string of battery troubles, faulty sets, difficulties about transport, rain, arrests, hide and seek with the Huns, lack of cash, flights at a moment's notice, false alarms, wicked treks over the mountains, laden like a mule, fright among one's collaborators, treachery, and friends getting shot. It is an atmosphere that all but paralyses work . . .

[In early March I] set off with M the Copper [Manoli Paterakis] and young GEORGE at dawn for BABYLON. The whole thing had been wonderfully laid on by G. I was dressed as a shepherd with top boots, sariki [turban] and cloak. Unfortunately, it was a boiling hot day, the only one that month, and I had to take the cloak off. At a little hut half way there, TWEEDLEDEE [Kostas Kastrinogiannes] was waiting, still in bed. We got him up, and made up my moustache and eyebrows with burnt cork – the dye wore off long ago – and he went forward on his bicycle to spy out the land. The roads were crammed with traffic, and there were streams of peasants going in for the end of the carnival (I had rather hoped to wander about Babylon in a funny hat and a false nose, making disguise unnecessary, but unfortunately it had been forbidden). On the right of the road we saw JOHN P [John Pendlebury, an SOE officer killed in Crete in 1941]'s grave. (It was just about where I last saw him during the trouble.) He is written up as 'J.P., Englischer Oberst, gefallen . . .' on a wooden cross.

The two miles from the bridge to the town were teeming with Huns and Itis – they seem to have posts all the way. G. pointed out the Greek Gestapo agents in undertones. TWEEDLEDUM [Aristeides Kastrinogiannes] rode forward to see that all was well at the TROJAN GATE [Canea Gate] (no pass control), rode back to give us the O.K. sign, and we passed through it with maddening slowness behind a donkey laden with faggots. There were about sixty Huns at the barbican, and it was a great moment when we got inside the city wall. The streets were seething with a carnival crowd, and our little procession of four made its way along the middle of the road, then down a lane to TWEEDLEDEE's house. Once inside, we all heaved a sigh, shook hands and burst out laughing. It was a great moment. None of us had slept all night, and we lay down and slept till dusk, and then made our way to PYLADES's house, where a huge spread was waiting, with gallons of wine, and GEORGE's principal helpers . . . It was a great evening.

I stayed there eight days, the busiest I have had in Crete. It was a huge succession of conferences all day with work far into the night. It was very exciting. There were Huns billeted in the houses on either side, drunk all the time, and you could hear nearly everything they said. It was wonderful having hot baths, breakfast in bed, and really good food. They put on the Ritz magnificently, and were unbelievably kind. We spent three gay evenings at NIMROD's (a grand man) with wine and song. I cut off the ends of my moustache (which was almost up to BO-PEEP's standards), borrowed a smart suit of TWEEDLEDUM's, put on a collar and tie, and was ye fyne olde Englishe Gentlemanne for the innumerable conferences. At dusk, only burnt-corked, I went for walks, to see the fishpond, the different important buildings, and the town defences. These last are pretty formidable; all the roads down to the sea front are blocked with walls eight or ten feet high, and three or four feet thick, with a small doorway; trenches are dug in the sand, and between them and the sea lies a jungle of wire among which land mines are sown. All cross roads have brick and cement MG [machine-gun] nests, some of them open at the top. The back streets and lanes have smaller brick MG nests, all open at the top. These are to be manned by machine gunners from the neighbouring houses, where the MGs or LMGs [light machine guns] are kept. Sten guns, grenades, and pistols are the obvious weapons to deal with these defences from inside.

When the time came to go, I borrowed a raincoat and a wonderful velvet trilby and bicycled out of the town with TWEEDLEDUM. I looked the image of a spy – just like the ones in the Careless Talk poster, I thought – but then, so do all Babylonians. My bike had a little tin swastika flag on the front. We sailed through the TROJAN GATE with the greatest of ease. LEONIDAS [another Cretan helper] was loitering in the road outside to see we got off safely and gave us a stage wink as we spun past. TWEEDLEDEE ran into a donkey and came off.

We biked out to AK's (the General's son's) country house, where GEORGE was waiting with my wardrobe, changed, had tea with AK's charming wife and then M the Cop and I set out for CAMELOT [Anogia] . . .

It was a wonderful week, and a great deal of business had been contracted. I felt as if I'd been taken on a new lease of life after all those months purely on the defensive. GEO[RGE] hurried back and launched the bill sticking campaign with PYLADES that night.

The Copper and I reached CAMELOT at three in the morning, in drenching rain – back to outlawry after the fleshpots of Egypt. STIFF [Ioannes Dramountanes] tumbled out of bed, roused his wife, and laid on a great feast with several of his pals dragged from their sleep, and SANCHO, just returned there from his recce; and we talked and drank and sang till dawn. My stay there lasted several days, and was a succession of feasts in the true CAMELOT tradition. TOM has left a great memory there, and all begged to have their greetings sent to him, which I do now . . .

I have been moving about a lot locally since my return at the end of March, but have made no big journeys. The locals are getting used to the Huns bit by bit – they didn't know them before here, and are beginning to realise that, when they wander from village to village, it's usually eggs, not English they are after.

German counter-espionage methods seem to have slipped back a bit. They have stacks of detailed information about TOM, XAN and me – our clothes, voices, whiskers, and idiosyncrasies, all of which are, naturally, quite different, and we have all been enquired after in a very practical way in the past. They have now sent round asking after a British officer of medium height and ordinary appearance who wanders about CRETE and sometimes calls himself YANNI, sometimes ALEKO, and sometimes MICHAEL . . .

Yesterday, an ME 109 [*sic*: probably an ME 110] flew very low, three times round SNOWDON [Mount Ida], with the rear gunner hanging out of his cockpit with binoculars. This Snowdon fixation is worth exploiting. When trouble is due to start, a party of men should go up there, firing off Verey flares for all they are worth everywhere, which will either send the Germans tooling up there in large numbers or put the wind up them thoroughly, and make them lock themselves indoors. The Huns did plenty of this kind of thing the year before last, and with everyone on our side, it will be possible to launch a really good *FRIGHT AND CONFUSION CAMPAIGN*. Carefully placed proclamations to be found by Huns from imaginary guerrilla leaders – BLACK DIMITRI, PANAGIOTI the GERMANOPHAGE, SIPHI of the RED BEARD etc., telling his followers to assemble at such and such a place – just where we want the Huns to be in fact. Notices in German (of carefully differentiated degrees of correctness, to make them appear from many different writers, and typed on different machines), polygraphed, addressing 'German soldiers!', and saying, 'It is with great difficulty that we are holding the Cretan Folk back from terrorist acts that clash with the Hague convention. But we warn you that, if you try their patience much more, we will be unable to control them', or 'G.S.! The hour of

Vengeance is at hand etc. etc', and signed: Captain YANNI in command of L section CRETE, or 'ALEKO, Capt. command of S. Sector', 'MICHAEL, Z Section', 'HARRY', 'NIKO', 'MONTY', and later other RICHARDS, PETERS, WILLIAMS etc. purely imaginary . . .

Here is a fruity one:

GERMANS!

You have now been two years in our island, and your rule has been the blackest stain on the pages of your already besmirched history. You have proved yourselves unfit to be considered as a civilised race, and infinitely worse than the Turks, who were noble enemies and men of honour.

You have proved yourselves savages, and as such you will be treated.

But not yet.

Wherever you go, Cretan eyes follow you. Unseen watchers dog your footsteps. When you eat and when you drink, when you wake and when you sleep, we are there watching you.

Remember!

The long Cretan knife makes no sound when it strikes between the shoulder blades.

Your time is running out. The hour of vengeance is drawing near.

Very near.

> Black Dimitri
> Archegos of Central Crete.

No exclamation marks or death's heads for this one (though plenty elsewhere) but a tone of deadly calmness.

This campaign needs laying on in a big way with care and psychological insight. Nothing would be more ludicrous or ineffective than a shoddy or half hearted one. We can get them in a state of jitters and nerves unmatched in history, because never has the stage been more propitiously set . . .

Please go through my telegrams and make a list of all the articles mentioned as being needed here, and send them in when you can. An important addition is: a number of small files for jailbreaks, and lethal (suicide) tablets. With these sewn in their clothes somewhere, and a revolver in their pockets, many agents would feel far happier, and equipped against whatever blow destiny might inflict.

It's three in the morning, and Matthew [White, SOE wireless operator] is leaving tomorrow. So here's an end.

Report No. 3

April to June 1943

Common topics in Leigh Fermor's third report, which he finished and sent out to Cairo in June 1943, remained enemy strength and spirits, local guerrilla politics, intelligence-gathering and propaganda work. Extracted here are three accounts of other matters: a German raid on his cliff-top headquarters (the 'Eagle's Nest'); the accidental death of his friend and guide Yanni Tsangarakis ('Sancho'), a young Cretan who had gone ashore with him a year earlier; and a discussion of the logistics of capturing a German coastal post.

~

HUN MORALE is as low as it could be. It is much as was described in other reports, but much aggravated by the fall of TUNIS and by the threatening leaflets dropped in early May. A practical demonstration of the radical change in Hun morale is the lack of sequels to the raid on my hideout. Here the Huns had concrete proof of the presence of British SS [Secret Service] work at its direst. A year – six months ago – they would have gone through the area with fire and sword leaving a trail of desolation and terror behind them. They used to do something of the kind if even an empty cartridge case was discovered. The total results in this case have been the arrest of two shepherds, who incidentally are from the wrong village and know nothing of the question concerned, and the ill treatment of one shepherd's wife . . .

Hun Raid on My HQ

This occurred in the following way . . . [On 11 April t]hree truck
loads [of German soldiers] arrived in KATZPHUR [Phourphouras]
. . . The [warning] blanket was laid out, but was unfortunately not
spotted. LOPEZ [Emmanuel Paradeisianos], as a secondary measure,
despatched young HIPPO [Hippokrates Antonakes] up the mountain to warn the chaps, and it is well he did. The Huns meanwhile
were making their way uphill by a different route, at a determined
pace. HIPPO found NIKO, BILL LEDGERWOOD [an Australian
soldier in Crete since 1941], BINGO [Corporal Bingham, an SOE
wireless operator] and MANOLI the MINOTAUR CALF
[Emmanuel Ntibirakes] cooking breakfast. The things were packed
up at high speed, in the middle of which the HUNS appeared
overhead. The M-CALF did great work hiding the wonderbox [the
wireless set] and battery. BINGO collected his code book and papers
– there were not many of these. I superintended a holocaust of all
MATT[hew White]'s old in and out cipherings before he left, and
all the vital stuff was hoisted out at high speed. M-CALF was
overhead, hiding a battery when the Huns came in sight, much
closer now, and one of them fired a pistol, which did not hit anyone.
The chaps set off down hill at full speed, clutching the essential
stuff. M-CALF was captured as he tried to break for it, HIPPO
had a narrow squeak, and jettisoned my attaché case in a bush,
hoping it would escape notice there, and got away. Unfortunately
it didn't. From a vantage point downhill, they saw twelve Huns,
with M-CALF in custody, go into the cave, and come out with
blankets, etc. At this point some of the HUNS spotted our chaps,
and started down hill after them. Our band made a dash to the
left, towards K., and got safely away . . .

About noon the Huns came down to KATZPHUR with
M-CALF laden with spoils. There were:

My attaché case
1 battery
Odd parts of the old W/T set

5 blankets (crawling [with lice])
Saucepan
Frying pan
Knives and Forks
BINGO's sheepskin coat (a Hun was wearing it)

I had gone through my attaché case most carefully before leaving. There could be no doubt from the contents as to what the owner's business was (were further evidence necessary) but no in or out messages, and not a single name of place or person even in the elaborate system of soubriquets that I always use. Nothing in fact that can give anyone away, or reveal any vital secret. The contents were:

An exercise book containing detailed Hun strengths in HERAKLION Nome (those contained in my last report) on the whole up to date till March, with a few sketch-maps.

A set of maps (unmarked)

140 sovereigns (I doubt if many of these found their way to the authorities)

90 Egyptian pounds

A sketch of HENRY (unnamed) in an old exercise book. Not a good likeness.

Some comic drawings of British military life, made for BILL's and BINGO's benefit.

An exercise book containing verses (my own in English) and others in French, German, Greek and Roumanian from memory.

A sketch of an imaginary Cretan mountaineer, bristling with weapons.

A long catalogue of arms covering seven sheets of foolscap, that I had amused myself by compiling one evening as the ideal amounts for all CRETE, if one had one's way. Most items run into six figures – rifles, tommy guns, 2" mortars, LMGs, A/Tk [Anti-Tank] rifles, fighting knives, MGs, pistols,

amm. of all kinds, cleaning materials, medical stores, binoculars, Verey pistols, flares, etc. etc. Nearly all the items
have a tick against them, made when I went through the
list trying to cut it down. The German impression will
certainly be that this huge quantity of arms is already in
CRETE, and it is a piece of involuntary propaganda of high
order.

Stationery.

1 compass, 1 pr. binoculars, .45 amm.

We got off very lightly. M-CALF being caught is the only thing
that worries me now. He is extremely tough and plucky, and I
don't think he will give anyone away. Every effort is being made
to get him out . . .

Everybody's conduct was exemplary, it seems, and by all accounts,
NIKO's especially so, showing great coolness in getting the essential stuff sorted out, hidden and carried off with the Huns well
within sight and range . . .

HIPPO, who helped M-CALF hide the set, went up a few
nights after the raid, and retrieved it. It was he who saved the
whole outfit from disaster, with LOPEZ and NIKO.

To my mind, the whole incident is a case of treachery, as it is
impossible to tumble on the Eagle's nest by chance. Opinions are
divided. The whole incident has now been digested, but its lessons
are not forgotten, and work goes on as usual once more . . .

SANCHO

I have got to record something tragic and horrible that happened
on the 25th of May. I did not inform GHQ [SOE HQ in Cairo]
of it before, as it could not possibly help matters, and I would
prefer you to learn just how it happened at the same time as you
learn [of] the event itself.

On the evening of the 25th of May I accidentally shot SANCHO,
and he died shortly afterwards.

It happened this way. We were sitting round the fire outside STIFF's sheepfold at CAMELOT at dusk (about 10 people in all) when news came that 300 Germans had arrived at CAMELOT, and were on their way to where we were. I told everyone to get packed up, and to take as many rifles as would go round. My rifle (a German one) had been brought from LOTUSLAND [the Amari valley] two days before by BILL. HERCULES [an assistant to MI6 officer Ralph Stockbridge] and one or two others had been cleaning them earlier in the day, before which I had unloaded mine and put the rounds back in the bandolier. It had been kept loaded near the door of the hut in case of trouble at night. Since then I had been working on the earlier part of this report some distance away, and had not seen that in the meanwhile most of the company, including 3 shepherd lads, cousins of STIFF's, had been amusing themselves by doing Greek and British arms drill with my rifle, and practising loading and unloading. At the time I'm speaking of, the rifles were all lying on their sides, newly oiled, with the bolts open, except mine, and I assumed they had been there since being cleaned in the morning. I drew the bolt back and forwards, easing the springs to see if it was working smoothly after being oiled (without realising it, I had put a round in the breach). I pressed the trigger and the round hit SANCHO, who was sitting by the fire a little distance doing up his sakouli, through the left hip. It looked a slight wound at first, and FISHY [Lieutenant Elevtherios Psaroudakes] and I bandaged him with field dressings, but on cutting his breeches open, we saw it had passed twice through his leg before entering the body. There were six wounds in all. We bound them up, but it was no use, and he died about an hour afterwards, shedding very little blood. He did not seem to suffer a great deal, and said some very kind words to me before he died that I shall never forget. Meanwhile, all the gear was hidden and sentries placed, in case the Germans came our way. Fortunately, they took another direction, towards CORNERS [Gonies], and encamped there. I had sent YANNAKO M, STIFF's cousin down to get Dr M., who arrived in the morning, several hours too late. It would have been useless anyway. We dug a grave about quarter of a mile away under a couple of ilex trees, and buried poor SANCHO soon after dawn, disguising the grave with stones and brambles.

Everyone was extremely decent to me about this horrible accident. No amount of writing will bring SANCHO back to life, or excuse my not examining the magazine before closing the bolt, and I am not going to attempt it. I should have known that Cretans are extremely lackadaisical about leaving firearms loaded at all times; this causes thousands of accidents of this type each year. Ironically enough, SANCHO did exactly the same thing with me at FLAILS last winter, in a hut with JO BRADLEY; but with a fortuitous three or four inches of difference. Everyone took the happening very philosophically, as if it were quite a common event. I could not, and cannot, do the same. SANCHO, during the year that we were almost constantly together, had certainly, with BEOWULF and the VICAR, become my best friend in CRETE, and he was equally certainly the best and hardest worker we have ever had here.

My intention was to go to STARLIGHT and tell SANCHO's family exactly what happened, as soon as the evacuation was finished. This caused a general outcry among all the eye witnesses, who said that it was out of the question, the situation in CRETE being what it is, and that the fact that SANCHO had been shot by me would cause untold trouble; not from his brothers and sisters, who are all friends of mine, but from other members of his family, and that his enemies would say I had shot him for treachery and blacken his name. This is not unlikely in CRETE. They then, led by SANCHO's cousin, LEONIDAS, FISHY . . . the DOCTOR, BEOWULF and STIFF fabricated a story, in which we were supposed to have run into a Hun ambush . . . and that SANCHO had been shot by a Hun while we tried to break for it. The whole party then took an oath that the truth should never come out. *Hic et ubique*, and that not even the revised version should be said till I gave the word. This is, as a matter of fact, the most sensible course, and I am going to adopt it. I want to say however that I did not agree to this hateful fiction out of a wish to shirk my responsibilities, but for the sake of SANCHO and his family, and our work in CRETE. When I get the chance, I am going to STARLIGHT to tell KANAKI and his other brothers that SANCHO was killed in the way agreed. This beastly sham is only permissible because the conditions here are so strange and unlike anything anywhere else . . .

S. was intending to undertake his [nephew CHARIDIMOS's] welfare in EGYPT, with his arrears of pay, which must amount to £200 odd. He was also planning to help his family – he is unmarried – who are very poor in CRETE. I hereby make it known that my arrears of pay up to £100 (till I get back) are at GHQ's disposal in anything that can help CH[ARIDIMOS] get settled into a job, or anything else he wants to do. If pensions are granted to the families of people who die in our work in CRETE, please lay this on for SANCHO. SANCHO was also recommended for a decoration (the most deserved in CRETE) by all of us. It would be a great thing if this could be sent to his family . . .

I am sorry for letting the firm down like this. It's all a very unhappy business. Actually, it will have no repercussions in CRETE, on our work or otherwise. I don't think I can say any more about this. What has happened has happened. Meanwhile there is a great deal of work to be done . . .

Capturing Hun Posts

These simple sounding operations are not nearly so easy as one would think. I have been in the MOUNTAINS of MORNE [Asterousia mountains] for four days now, where I came for the sole purpose of laying on a raid on a Hun post. I have some thirty men under arms arriving in a couple of days.

The factors that make this small operation such a teaser are: –

(i) You can't afford to have firearms banging off indiscriminately if a party is landing and there is important stuff to be transported inland, as the neighbouring posts will hear the din and warn the inland garrisons by telephone (the actual post of course will have its lines cut); and make the descent to and crossing of BADLANDS by a landed party complete with donkey loads of batteries, charges, W/T sets, and assorted gear, a very tricky matter.

(ii) You can't afford to risk the safe evacuation of your party of evacuees containing women and children (to which, I understand, the taking of the post is a secondary matter).

(iii) The post has got to have a suitable hide-out nearby to contain a party of fifty – near enough for self and thugs to approach post (which can only be done after dark) on tiptoe, take the post by a brisk *coup de main*, march the prisoners down to the evacuation point (which may not be nearby), RV with the women and children, embark them (assuming the ship turns up just at the right moment), load your stuff on donkeys and set off for the hinterland, all under cover of a short summer night. Next morning, all the Huns in the area will be on the warpath, and there is little cover and few friends in the BADLANDS, where day will break on you. You couldn't remain in the MORNE MOUNTAINS, as the Huns would be raking every cave and cranny for a week afterwards.

(iv) If the Huns should hear your approach, ensconce themselves, and say 'Do your damnedest', you haven't got the weapons to do an awful lot, but you might manage all right. If they hold out till dawn, you're done for, as far as capture goes, as the ship has to be off under cover of darkness, and nothing would be more ludicrous than an abortive attack.

All these difficulties are minor matters which I am quite ready to risk trusting in surprise and a good dose of luck on the right side. But things become difficult indeed if you can't find a local guide with the guts and the sporting spirit to help you. You can't make a recce by day, as the coast is forbidden and a stranger wandering near the post, and noting down just where the land-mines are, is liable to be shot at. They would probably miss, but they will be on their guard, and this may not only botch the attack, but the evacuation as well, and a recce by yourself in these dark nights, among rocks where you lose yourself in two minutes, is a hopeless concern. You *must* have a good guide, to be really abreast of the lay of the land, and the whole thing might be [a] frightful mess without this knowledge.

BATTISTA [Agios Ioannes] is the post that sounded most promising. It is far away from all the others and when I heard that there was a spirited 27 year old shepherd six foot high and a great lad by repute, who had his sheep just outside the post – the only one of the area who is allowed down there, and who frequently sleeps in the post itself, it all seemed too easy. My plan was the following (own tps. [troops], 30 odd men with rifles or pistols, 3 sub-machine guns, 6 grenades. Inf. about the enemy – 15 men living in a chapel built into a cave at the end of a gully running 300 inland from the sea, accessible by a coast path (mines sown at one or two points) and by a path from the mountain above, passing fifty feet exactly over the chapel. Two sentries and 2 MGs. outside the little wall that encloses the chapel at night).

To send three men above the chapel, to cut the wire and stand by. To steal along the gully, and, if the sentries were not at their posts (as is possible) to walk straight in with a tommy gun and a crowd of thugs, and make a stick-up. If the sentries were at their posts, to creep as near as possible, throw a Mills bomb at them to drive them inside, or kill them (if the ground was too open to creep up on them and knock them out), follow them up if surprise was complete, shout over the wall in German that they were now British Prisoners of war, that the invasion had started, and that I was anxious to save them from the brutal Cretans. Any of these tactics would work, backed up by shouts in English from all round and above (they would be informed that the post was surrounded). If they still didn't budge they would be informed that a mountain gun had been unloaded from the destroyer, and would shell the post to powder if they did not surrender at once. All this is assuming that the first surprise entry was impossible, and any of them would succeed. The Huns are in no fighting mood in these posts, and would surrender at once to the smallest force of English rather than be left to the Cretans. I planned to make great use of drop flares, dropping them in front of the chapel from above, if they should be stubborn, to add to the confusion and bewilderment. One can only form rough plans for this sort of blind operation, adapting the detail to suit the circumstances. Surprise and determination are obviously one's main weapons.

But the shepherd turned out to be a huge lout with frightened eyes like a hare. Not only did he refuse to guide us, but, after a whole night of reasoning, wheedling, promising and praising, he went off to his village and pretended to be ill, in order to be out of our reach, saying before he went, that a new post had just been installed at ZINC [unidentified location], why not take that? I interviewed three others with the same disheartening results, and rather than jeopardise the party by talking to any more, shook the dust of that village off my feet, and made my way to ZINC, where I discovered that the post was a fiction to get me and my dangerous plans out of the area. It was no use repeating: 'We'll leave a letter saying it's the work of commandos, and announce it on the wireless so that no Cretan will suffer', again and again. The answer always came 'The Germans will burn our village down' (which is nonsense). I was sitting in a state of cold rage above ZINC when your telegram reached me cancelling the operation . . .

Report No. 4

June and July 1943

Scribbled with the promise of an imminent Royal Navy pick-up, Leigh Fermor's fourth report was particularly rushed. In the moments available, he brought Cairo quickly up to date with his work in Heraklion and described an abortive attempt with two Cretans to sabotage enemy shipping in the harbour. The report was written, too, as news was reaching him of brutal enemy reprisals. These were being inflicted on the Cretan population in response to recent lightning attacks by British raiding forces on an airfield at Kastelli and a petrol dump at Peza.

~

11 July 1943

I have got about an hour in which to write my whole report, so here goes . . .

MORALE

Hun. Very, very low.

Local. Very high until the sabotage executions took place when it fell to rock bottom; the British came in for much cursing . . .

. . . SABOTAGE

. . . I went into Babylon by bike, staying with some friends of
Cop Manoli over a café, got the toys brought in by donkey, and
leased a house near the harbour . . . Later I biked out and contacted
the PEZA unit [the British raiding force tasked with attacking the
petrol dump], who supplied me with some essential toys for the
limpets. I got back next day, rigged the things up in the house,
and set out with the Copper and Minoan Mike [Michael
Akoumianakes]. We got into the harbour, crawled towards the
sea, and were stopped by a lot of broken planes, over, under or
through [which] there was no crawling without raising a terrific
clatter of tin that set the sentries on the move. Minoan Mike left
us at that point. The cop and I spent the rest of the next night
trying to find a way through, creeping at snail's pace behind
sentries using what cover we could. But there was no way through
from there without killing two of them, which would have made
our retreat impossible. We ended up with one three yards off, the
other ten . . . both flashing torches. Spent about two hours not
daring to move a muscle, and finally, alas, had to withdraw. I'm
sorry about this, but we had a damn good try.

We got back to the house, slept till dawn, then back to our
friend above the café. The whole town was in a scare next morning,
when the results at PEZA and KASTELLI were known. Arrests
began at once in the provinces. We got out by car just before
they started at Babylon. Shooting started next day. 50 in all that
nome, none elsewhere . . .

I hope the service of this [raiding] activity to our general strategy
has been high, because here it has caused much havoc to morale,
and caused much anti-British feeling . . .

No time for more now, the boat leaves tonight.

Report No. 5

July to September 1943

*Another rushed affair, Leigh Fermor's next report was concerned mainly
with updating Cairo on recent discussions with Italian officers on Crete
(Mussolini had fallen in July and an Italian surrender seemed imminent).
The report also described a visit that he made to the mountain hideout
of Manoli Bandouvas, the Cretan guerrilla leader who, at considerable
cost to the local populace, would come out briefly to fight the Germans
in September.*

*Reproduced below, Leigh Fermor's account of his visit to Bandouvas
('Bo-Peep' in the report) provides a colourful snapshot of guerrilla life in
Crete. It also illuminates some of the more brutal tasks with which British
personnel on the island were occasionally confronted: during his time with
Bandouvas, Leigh Fermor helped preside over the trials and death sentences
of captured Cretan traitors. It was during this period, too, that Leigh
Fermor arranged for an arms drop of weapons and other warlike stores
with which Bandouvas could be equipped.*

~

2 September 1943

I'm afraid that this report, like the last one, must be written in
great haste. I have been too busy lately to sit down and write it,
and had intended to get it written during the days spent lying-up
on the way to the beach. Unfortunately I have been suddenly
attacked by a plague of large sores and boils all over my legs which

make walking very painful, so I will not be able to take charge of Tom's reception party as I wished, and must get my report written somehow before the chaps leave . . .

Bo-Peep

There is no doubt that this curious man has caught the CRETAN fancy, and wields a more wide-spread influence in the masses than any other single leader in Crete.

I visited his lair last month for three reasons:

a) It was the only spot in Tuscany that I could think of at an hour's notice where I could send the [wireless] set to be on the spot in case things developed quickly between the Huns and the Itis.
b) I wanted to superintend the [supply] drop in person.
c) I wanted to see just what was going on.

The climb up to SODOM [the Vianno plateau] (where the arms were dropped) took five hours. COPPER and I slept at a sheep fold, and pushed on upwards another three hours, on to the roof of the TUSCAN [Lasithi] mountains. We were stopped by a dozen brigand sentries, and finally reached BO-PEEP's lair under a large escort.

The lair is a complete improvised village of branch-woven huts, on a rocky slope from where you can see, miles below, the whole of TUSCANY as far as EOTHEN [Seteia] stretched out like a map. It was midday, and BO-PEEP and his toughs – a hundred of them – were eating under a huge ilex-tree. Whiskery embraces began.

A superb wigwam was built for me by GRIGORI [Grigorios Khnaras] and his lads, and I settled down to see what was happening.

The band is the most heteroclite assembly imaginable. Large numbers of hairy shepherds and mountaineers, a few army Officers, a handful of communists, fugitives, a priest, two monks from

UPPER JOSEPH [Apano Siphi], both festooned with cartridge belts, a few very young men in student hats, some toughs from ASIA MINOR, men from every part of CRETE, countless policemen, real and bogus, in uniform, two young men in Hun uniform, several ATHENIANS and stranded Greek soldiers from the mainland, two Australians, one New Zealander, and an enormous Cossack called PIETR, escaped from the Russian prison Camp at Ay. GALINI, quite silent except in explaining that he is not a communist . . .

I was there about ten days, and people kept streaming up every day, till there were about 160 by the time I left. There is an extremely well-supplied store cave, a tailor, a baker, a cobbler, a carpenter and various other 'tradesmen' who are always busy. 'Guards' are changed regularly, with sentries at three look-out points. From a tactical point of view, the place is as safe as anywhere in the island, with a huge mountain on one side, and almost sheer cliffs on the other three, the whole well camouflaged by trees. The store cave is kept filled by voluntary contributions from the neighbouring villages, and there is apparently sufficient for six months. The armament was pitiful and inadequate, every kind of rifle being in evidence, including one sporting gun and one muzzle-loader. They all have a blind adoration of BO-PEEP, who rules over them, and all the surrounding district, like a fatherly but autocratic oriental voivode. I can't help liking BO-PEEP, in spite of all his misdeeds, and am certain that with right handling, he will play the game. There is no doubt that he can summon a force of several thousand at three days' notice, and, under our orders. This is not to be sneezed at . . .

A baby was toted up on a mule which we baptised together, thus becoming God-mothers. The poor thing was christened ANGLIA EPANASTASIS (England Revolution . . .).

We had many talks . . . He wants his men to wear British cap badges, not GREEK (nor Irish Guards!) and is eager to have his band considered as a unit of the British Army. I'm all for this. I gave him a long pi-jaw on the responsibilities of wearing British uniform, especially after the incident described below.

I had left the lair with BO-PEEP for a meeting with MAURICE [Lieutenant Colonel Nikolaos Plevres] some hours away. During our absence, one of BO-PEEP's anti-traitor squads captured a famous local traitor, L——, who had been let out of prison by the Huns to find and betray CRETANS with rifles. This he had done to some purpose. When they got him to the lair, they started torturing him, and HARRY [Harry Brooke, Leigh Fermor's wireless operator], summoned by shouts of anguish, left his hut, and found a ring of CRETANS round L—— who was hanging by his legs from the branch of a tree. He immediately ordered them to take him down, and had him put under a guard till I got back, for which he deserves full marks. When we got back, I made the hell of a row (soldiers, not barbarians, all we are fighting against etc.). BO-PEEP, HARRY and I then presided over a trial, he was found guilty, taken out, and shot.

The next day GEO. S—— – the man who also betrayed the caique that the Huns sank South of SELINO in March full of Officers escaping to EGYPT – was captured at pistol point (on leave from CANEA in his village of PEVKOI), hauled up to the lair, tried, and publicly executed after a full confession, giving many names that I am sending to XAN.

This anti-traitor and Gestapo drive is working excellently. About fifteen have been liquidated in BABYLON nome during the last months. Every day BO-PEEP sends out a party – varying in numbers from three to twenty – to distant villages [to try to seize them] . . . Others are ambushed and shot with Tommy-guns. One was strangled on the main road, then carried a mile on the assassin's shoulder, and dumped in a ditch. In time this should put a stop to treachery in this area . . .

THE ARMS DROP

This was an unqualified success. The plane came very low indeed, flashed greetings from the wing tips in answer to the flares that were joyfully thrown in the air by COPPER, and the chutes sailed gracefully down among the [signal] fires, the whole lot falling within a radius of a hundred and fifty yards. SODOM was entirely surrounded by a hundred gangsters to keep possible Huns at bay. Several could not resist firing feu-de-joie. It was indeed magnificent. Shouts of 'Zeto e Anglia!' rent the night sky . . .

Only a few rifles were damaged in one container whose chute failed to open. The others were in perfect condition. The administration was excellent. The heavy ones were unpacked at once, entered up in a ledger by an Officer, loaded up, and sent up to the den, where a large storehouse had been prepared. The smaller ones went up intact and were opened in my presence, and fairly distributed. Large numbers are now in bush shirts, with cap-comforters on their heads, belts and bayonets, and look very well. There were several omissions, mentioned in my telegrams. Coats and battledress will be needed in the winter, and BO-PEEP has himself made out a list of further requirements, which is fairly sensible. My contention is that his gang is worth backing. It was like BO-PEEP's birthday, and, as I stated, the whole affair was the best bit of propaganda in CRETE so far . . .

I'm afraid this report is far from coherent or well put together. I have had blood-poisoning for the last week, have eaten scarcely anything, and feel bloody. I hope you'll treat this as an excuse.

Report No. 6

September 1943

Events in Crete moved fast in the autumn of 1943. Written while still on the island, Leigh Fermor's sixth report was principally an account of his continued dealings with local Italian officers – especially Lieutenant Franco Tavana, an energetic and stridently anti-Fascist counter-espionage officer – after the sudden announcement on 8 September of Italy's surrender. It describes the local negotiations between the Italians and Germans and his own efforts to persuade Italian units to retain some cohesion and give their weapons to the Cretans, even as strong German forces went about disarming and dispersing them, and closes with his arrangements for the escape from the island of General Angelo Carta. It was while assisting with the final stages of Carta's flight that Leigh Fermor found himself stranded aboard the Royal Navy vessel sent to pick Carta up, and was shipped to Egypt, too.

~

21 September 1943

The Italian Armistice and After

. . . [T]wo days before the armistice my operator (S/Sgt. BROOKE) was off the air owing to heavy and continual rain. The only hideout I had been able to find close to TUSCANY, and at the same time to SODOM for the parachutists and the

MORNE MTS for boating parties, was a bleak, shelterless hillside on the western slopes of the TUSCAN Mts above CASTLES [Kastelli Pediados]. We sat there and got soaked to the skin for thirty-eight hours on end, making frequent, slippery and vain efforts to get on the air and keep the rain out of the set at the same time. I finally received your message, warning me that the armistice was pending, and the other telling me of its fulfilment, on the morning of the eighth. A few minutes later a shepherd arrived from the plain, foaming with excitement, with the same news, and also told us that the Huns had visited the Iti post at MOUCHTAROU at dawn and stripped the Itis of all their arms. I assumed the same thing (or Italian armed resistance) had probably started in LASITHI, and, in view of your wish to get the Iti arms handed over to the Cretans, had to move fast . . .

The problem of the arms handover was a difficult one . . . I had [previously] gone to certain lengths to stiffen the Itis' inclination to resist Hun disarmament, to remain united, and to hit back, on express orders from you. On the same orders I had also held out some hopes of allied support in the event of an armed clash. Thus my new mission insisting they should tamely give their arms to the Greeks – a course which would obviously lead to heavy penalties on Itis and Greeks alike . . . – was no enviable one . . .

MINOAN MIKE arrived at my mountain that night with an Italian soldier, and a cargo of assorted arms sent by TAVANA. He had fixed up an Iti motor car to wait for me in the Tuscan plain. We went down next day and rattled along the VILLENEUVE [Neapolis] Road. Half way there we were met by TAVANA in the General's car on his way out to see if anything had gone wrong. He was dressed in a most dashing Alpine uniform with spurs and plumes and a phenomenal number of medal ribbons. I changed over to his car and we rolled into VILLENEUVE in state, and arrived in his house in time for an excellent dinner, washed down by chianti.

TAVANA was in tremendous spirits and expecting the [Allied] invasion at every moment, and discussing what dispositions the Itis should take up. This was the result of my former line of talk, and I felt like several different kinds of swine for having led them up the garden path. He had already tipped off all his officer friends to make a resolute resistance to any Hun attempts to disarm them. He has an attractive and eager personality and great popularity and respect among all ranks in TUSCANY. I informed him that plans had changed, that since the invasion of Italy Crete operations were no longer immediate. He naturally said it was out of the question to hand over all their arms to the Cretans, but that he would do what he could on the quiet.

I insisted on seeing the General [Carta], and after dark he went round to his house and smuggled him along unobserved by the newly arrived Gestapo men. He is plump, rosy, urbane and very agreeable. He said that MÜLLER had visited him the day before, and demanded that all arms should be handed over. CARTA refused and eight hours of talk followed without any result . . .

[W]hen the General had tiptoed home to bed, TAVANA and I sat up till daybreak discussing what we could do on the side in the way of arms. We decided to get whatever surplus arms we could smuggled to outlying points by car, and taken over by responsible local leaders and distributed at once. It was very tricky, however, as Huns were continually arriving and nearly all dumps were under their supervision. During the following days, however, we managed to hand over about 200 rifles, quantities of grenades and ammunition, a couple of mortars, and several LMGs and MGs. This was mostly done by TAVANA himself, driving a lorry out after dark, dismissing the sentry, loading the stuff on board with his soldier-servant, and driving it to the approved tryst. He is certainly a spirited young man. His first action when the news of the armistice came through was to burn every bit of paper in his archives. When the Huns took over, they would have found not a shred of guidance to help and would have to begin from the start – no easy matter at this late hour . . .

The Huns continued stripping Italian troops of all but their personal arms, summoning them to Neapolis, and sending them westwards to the various destinies that awaited them . . .

I was now anxious to save what I could from this steady erosion and, rightly or wrongly, decided to save the General, who had not behaved too badly, to send to you for information purposes (also Capt. LUDOVICI his ADC) and above all Capt. GROSSI from the 3rd Bureau (ops) for the same reason, and obtain, if possible, the plans of the heavy defences of LASITHI in detail, as I felt sure the Huns would not change them . . .

Meanwhile VILLENEUVE was filling up with Huns . . . and a swarm of plain clothes spies. I was living in TAVANA's house and almost every hour receiving panicky letters from our leaders in the town, to escape before it was too late. The Huns paid one visit to the house, while I was there alone, in search of TAVANA. I spent an uncomfortable half hour under a bed, clutching my revolver, and swallowing pounds of fluff and cobwebs. I finally left in a civvy car . . . and stayed at the OUTRIVER [unidentified location] (on the road between VILLENEUVE and the TUSCAN plain) . . . TOM was by this time near at hand with the [wireless] set, between which and me COPPER MANOLI had been speeding with streams of messages . . . I started organising the General's flight, and urging TAVANA by letter to get his hands on to the defence maps.

He arrived next morning in the General's car, stopped outside the village and sent in MINOAN MIKE to fetch me. I found him beaming under a plane tree with a whole satchelful of documents. They were the full defence organisation of LASITHI, a map of the points considered most valuable to different kinds of attack, and much besides. I took it back to the village feeling it might go off bang on the way. I can't help feeling that this result justifies all the fuss and anxiety and frustration of the preceding few days. I also managed to secure an up-to-date Italian map (4/9/43) indicating the location of guerrilla bands in Greece and a fascinating translation of a secret Hun document dealing with the battle and Hun occupation of CRETE up till the end of ANDRAE's administration. It is a long confession of guilt and ends up with some absorbing paragraphs on British activity in Crete . . .

The flight of CARTA and his officers was laid on with the help of an excellent GK [Greek] Captain . . . They left in the

General's car and a lorry (filled with arms; TAVANA was game to the last!) . . . [then] walked across the TUSCAN plain, the General's car, with pennant flying, leaving at once for SETEIA, where it was to be abandoned on the road as a false scent. COPPER, GRIGORI and I met the party in the village near TUSCANY, and took them by long and arduous stages across the mountains and the plain to the MORNE MOUNTAINS, where I am writing this report in conditions of acute discomfort . . .

When we halted, CARTA and I would drink some of the excellent Triple Sec in his water bottle, and he would regale me with lively anecdotes of high life in Rome and Paris or his reminiscences as an MFH in Trieste. He is most informative and entertaining on the subject of BRÄUER and MÜLLER and German officers in general. He went with a great swing everywhere. He has always been a popular figure in LASITHI.

On the second day of our journey Hun recce. planes (FIESELER STORCHS) flew low all over the mountains we were crossing, dropping leaflets (enclosed). They fell right at our feet. They were offers, in German, Italian and Greek of thirty million drachmas reward for General CARTA, dead or alive, and a full pardon for any evildoer or outlaw who would hand him over. CARTA was very amused.

The abduction of CARTA made the Huns boil with anger. Search parties were sent out everywhere, and all garrisons told to try and apprehend him before he left the island. The nuisance value is considerable and I advise you to exploit this, announcing his escape on the wireless, even letting him talk against the Huns on it. It will make the Huns more awestruck than ever at the long arm of the Secret Service, which already has great bogey value . . .

I realise by your telegrams that you consider him something of a white elephant. I hope he will not prove so, and that you will manage to get a lot of useful stuff out of them all told. Treat them as well as is allowed. If only for his good administration of TUSCANY in sharp contrast to that of the Huns he is worth some consideration . . .

Report No. 7

February and March 1944

As explained in 'Abducting a General', Leigh Fermor returned to Crete by parachute in February 1944 but had to wait seven weeks for Billy Moss and the rest of his team to join him. It was a frustrating period, albeit spent in the agreeable company of another SOE officer, Sandy Rendel.

Leigh Fermor penned his seventh report on the eve of Moss's arrival by boat. Aside from bringing Cairo up to date on the abduction plans – it was now that he learned that General Müller had been replaced – Leigh Fermor added a little about his own recent work with Rendel, which included ordering the killing of another Cretan traitor. The report ends with a description of how he and Rendel, together with their wireless operator and Cretan guides, experienced an uncomfortably close shave with German troops on the eve of Moss's arrival.

~

Monastery of the 12 Apostles,
near CASTELLIANA
30th March, 1944

. . . [M]y time in Crete has been almost entirely taken up by waiting for the rest of my party to arrive, and a tedious business it has been. I have been a guest since my arrival in SANDY's area, and a most patient and friendly host he has proved . . .

My Operation

This has had many discouraging setbacks in its early stages, both in our lateness in arriving in Crete, and then only in driblets, and in the frequent absences of the quarry. But if BILL and the other lads and the equipment arrive tonight, it looks as if our chances are as good as ever. Though the original quarry has left, he has been replaced . . . so I intend to try and get him as soon as possible. The necessity of my presence in the drop ground excluded the making of recces. in the snatch area, so don't expect results at once. I am going to try and pull it off as quickly as possible, however . . .

Execution

Last month a posse of MPANTOUVAS' gang arrived at the limeri [sheepfold], bringing with them . . . a renowned LASITHI traitor . . . I and SANDY ordered his immediate liquidation and he was carted off and shot in a cave at once. Good riddance . . .

Monastery of the 12 Apostles, near Castelliana

The Abbot of this Monastery deserves great credit. This morning SANDY, JOHN [Stanley, Inter-Services Liaison Department] and I, and our guides, were sitting in the one guest room of this small and primitive monastery, when a party of seven Germans arrived. They were one minute's distance from the front door before they were spotted. The Abbot at once opened a trap door leading to the cellar, through which we all piled, and lay there holding our breath while the Germans stamped in two feet over our head. The Abbot entertained and fed them for two hours with the utmost coolness and sangfroid. We could see them through the chinks in the floor boards. They finally left, convinced that their host was a law-abiding germanophile, and we emerged from our priests' hole. It was a very near thing for all of us, and the situation was only saved by the Abbot's presence of mind and pluck. He is Archimandrite THEOPHYLAKTOS . . .

3rd April, 1944 . . .

. . . Nothing to say yet beyond the few notes in my very mucky and hasty report. Hope BILLY and the lads arrive tonight; it has been a very trying wait . . .

Report No. 8

'Short Report on Capture of Gen Kreipe', May 1944

Safely aboard the launch that left Crete with General Kreipe on the evening of 14 May 1944, Leigh Fermor and his colleagues reached the Egyptian coast a few hours later, docking safely at Mersa Matruh. Kreipe was immediately handed over to the British military authorities, which soon had him on his way to England for interrogation. (Contrary to other published accounts, this took place on his arrival in England, not in Cairo.)

For his part, Leigh Fermor was promptly incapacitated in Egypt with what was diagnosed as polyarthritis. Three months in hospital followed. It was in hospital that the insignia of the Distinguished Service Order, awarded for his role in the abduction, was pinned to his battledress tunic (he wore the tunic over his pyjamas). It was also in hospital that Leigh Fermor wrote the following report. Written in a tone more consistently military than that adopted in most of his other reports, it describes the build-up to the kidnap, the execution of the abduction and the successful evacuation of the abductee, and is Leigh Fermor's most contemporary account of the deed.

~

16 May 1944

On Feb 4th I dropped into CRETE on the KATHARO Plateau, LASITHI PROVINCE, and made a good landing. Captain MOSS, Stanley, of the Coldstream Guards, and the two CRETANS that formed the rest of the party were unable to follow, owing to the sky suddenly clouding. They came back on seven nights during the next two months but the weather was consistently bad, and after several sea attempts, they finally landed at SOUTSOURO on the 4th April.

Our orders were to capture the GERMAN General Commanding the 22nd SEBASTOPOL (BREMEN) Div., then General MÜLLER. Shortly before MOSS's arrival with the remainder of the party, MÜLLER was withdrawn from that Command and replaced by General KREIPE, who had served in FRANCE and on the LENINGRAD and KUBAN fronts.

We and our party, now seven strong, struck North across MONOFATSI and PEDIADA counties, and established a HQ in the mountains above KOSTAMONITZA. I then left for HERAKLION in shepherd costume to recce the area Michael AKOUMIANAKIS our HERAKLION agent and I had chosen as the most likely one. This lay at PT. 1727 at the junction of the ARCHANES road and the HOUDETSI–HERAKLION road, where a sharp twist in the road would force any vehicle to slow up considerably. This was the most suitable place on the road from ARCHANES (KREIPE's Div. HQ) and KNOSSOS, where he lived at the VILLA ARIADNE. Several days' recce proved that he left his house any time between dusk and 9 o'clock. The plan was formed to carry out the operation on this return journey, under cover of darkness.

Three difficulties were: –

(i) To be sure of not mistaking another car for the General's.
(ii) Disposing of any other vehicle and its occupants should they pass during the Op[eration].
(iii) Avoiding bringing down reprisals on the local population.

The first was obviated by placing an agent (ELIAS ATHANASSAKIS) to acquaint himself thoroughly with the shape of the car, size of black-out slits on headlamps etc. He did this excellently. The second difficulty was to be dealt with by using a small ANDARTES Band, to capture the passengers and ditch any traffic that made an untoward appearance. The third problem was more difficult, and I left HERAKLION (where I spent two nights) for HQ at KOSTAMONITZA, where Capt. MOSS, M. AKOUMIANAKIS and I had a conference and worked out a plan. As the operation planned out exactly as we laid our scheme in every detail except one (the abolition of the Partisan Band at the last moment), I will not go over it twice.

When the plan was arrived at, I summoned ATHANASIOS BOURDZALIS, a good Patriot from ASIA MINOR, with a band of 15 CRETAN ANDARTES, to our HQ, added them to our party of 9 and moved Westwards with them by night on the 19th/20th April, spending the next day at KHARASSO (Map Ref: 2829), reaching our final hideout near SKALANI, among the trees and reeds of a dried up river bed at Map Ref: 1829, 20 minutes' march from the proposed site of the Op. The party turned out to be too large for effective concealment in this rather dangerous and traitorous area near HERAKLION, and we unwillingly sent the Partisans back, none of whom were in the picture, on most friendly terms, and decided to carry out the Op with a party of 9 picked men, on a nucleus of our own immediate followers 2 or 3 years in the service. We then lay up and waited for the right moment. This was one of the most trying parts of the Op. Four evenings running he [Kreipe] came back before dusk, as if he had got wind of the plan. On the fifth, however, night fell and he was still at his Div. HQ, so Capt. MOSS and I put on German police-corporal uniforms, and hastened with our party to the road-fork. ELIAS was posted near ARKHANES to signal one torch flash at the approach of the car (2 flashes if accompanied) to a scout posted nearer us who was to signal down half a kilometre of flex to an electric bell, next to another scout who was to flash the signal to us. MOSS and I took up our positions as traffic MPs in the road, the men (who knew each detail of the drill by heart) were hidden in ditches either side of the road-fork.

At 9:30 the warning signal flash came, and three minutes later the car came slowly round the bend. MOSS and I waved red lamps up and down, and the car stopped, and we walked towards the two doors drawing our pistols. I opened the right door of the car, flashed the torch inside, and saw the General was sitting beside the Chauffeur. He was easily recognisable by his tabs, medals and Iron Crosses. I asked for his papers in GERMAN, and while he was explaining, MOSS opened the other door, struck the driver hard with a life preserver, took him by the shoulders, threw him out to the waiting CRETANS, who quickly disarmed, handcuffed and bound him, and started off for the hills. MOSS then jumped into the driver's seat.

My party and I simultaneously seized the General, handcuffed and bound him, and put him in the back of the car. PATERAKIS, TYRAKIS and SAVIOLAKIS jumped in beside him, with three sub-machine guns stuck out of the windows, and had the General covered by two fighting-knives.

The rest of the party dispersed at once; I put on the General's hat and sat in his seat beside MOSS, who started up the engine and headed for HERAKLION. The whole halt and operation took just over a minute, and the CRETANS carried out their parts like clockwork. A car and three troop-trucks passed us two minutes after starting up, so we had done it in the nick of time.

We drove on past SPILI KNOSSOS, and TEKE, into HERAKLION market-square, then through the CANEA Gate, the main GERMAN post in HERAKLION, and out along the RETIMO road. We passed 22 road-blocks in all. The sentry at one attempted to stop us by waving his torch up and down, but MOSS drove straight on at the same speed. Other sentries saluted or stood to attention when they saw the two pennants of the car. We chose this route as being the most improbable one and the least likely to arouse suspicion: in this we were not wrong.

We drove for about an hour and a half to YENI GAVE (MR: 870370) where MOSS, PATERAKIS and SAVIOLAKIS got out with the General, who was then unbound (having volunteered his word of honour not to escape nor to draw attention to himself in the event of GERMANS being near). After the first shock he seemed to accept the 'fait accompli' fatalistically, and I informed him that he was an honourable prisoner of war captured by BRITISH Officers and would be treated as such. That party, under MOSS, then set off up the foothills of Mount IDA in the direction of ANOYEIA, a large and patriotic mountain village. I then drove the car on with TYRAKIS to a point between CHELIANA (MR: 835375) and MOURDZANA, where a footpath runs Northward to a suitable submarine beach at AMYRA (ISLD [Inter-Services Liaison Department, a cover-name for MI6] did actually make a landing here last year).

We left a sealed letter addressed to General BRÄUER and all GERMAN authorities in CRETE (appended), stating that the General had been taken prisoner by BRITISH Officers shortly before, and by the time the letter was read, would be on his way to Cairo.

We then abandoned the car without destroying it, and left a BRITISH overcoat inside as corroborative detail. By this process we hoped to exculpate the CRETANS living near the scene of abduction, of suspicion. The ruse was successful. We then struck southward towards ANOYEIA and reached it as dawn broke. My GERMAN uniform caused looks of hate in this notoriously lawless village. During the afternoon planes patrolled the Northern coast constantly and a Fieseler-Storch hovered for three hours over every peak and ravine in Mount IDA, dropping hastily turned-out leaflets stating General KREIPE had been captured by bandits, that his whereabouts could not be unknown to the population and that, unless he was surrendered within three days, all the local villages of HERAKLION Province would be razed to the ground and the sternest measures brought to bear on the civilian population.

It is to the lasting credit of the CRETANS that, though hundreds (till he was eventually evacuated) knew his whereabouts, the secret was loyally kept. Indeed our progress was a kind of royal procession of enthusiasm and congratulation.

MOSS's party and mine contacted at nightfall and we set off

with an escort of ANOYEIANS and the General on a route up the steep Northern slopes of IDA, till we reached the lair of MICHAEL XYLOURIS' band of Partisans.

The Party detailed to conduct the GERMAN driver across MONOPHATSI Province to the same RV arrived soon after, but without the driver who had been so badly hit and walked so slowly that he had to be disposed of on the way owing to the hue and cry in the plains.

Next day we marched right over the top of Mt IDA through deep snow (one of the most difficult and arduous climbs in CRETE which the General performed on foot), exchanging our bodyguard of XYLOURIS' men for a party belonging to PETRAKO-GEORGIS' band half-way. Advance scouts sent down the Southern slope of the mountain lit a series of beacon fires to show that the way was clear as ugly rumours of GERMAN concentrations in the AMARI below us were beginning to come in. A thousand GERMANS spread over the foothill villages was the most-named figure. We fetched up in a labyrinthine cave and remained there all next day. Morale continued to be extremely high.

About here our troubles began. Our carefully planned RV with Major DUNBABIN fell through as he was down with malaria somewhere in the AMARI and the charging-engine of his set with XYLOURIS' Band was out of order. Runners were sent hot-foot to three other sets, two in Western RETIMO Province, the other (RENDEL's) far to the East near HIERAPETRA in LASITHI. But communications were very long and it was many days before we got an answer from any of them, and then the plans outlined were out of date and the quickly changing situation made them impossible anyway.

We managed by an intricate system of posts along the foothills to slip our heavily armed caravan through the cordons and reached AYIA PARASKEVI, hoping to escape from SAKHTOURIA beach, a night's march SW of here. The day after we arrived, however, SAKHTOURIA village was burnt to the ground and most of the male population arrested owing to a gun-running operation there three weeks before, in which no less than 30 mules, laden with rifles, had fanned out all over Central CRETE. We could also hear the explosions and see the smoke of the villages of LOCHRIA, KAMARES and MARGARIKARI being bombed and blown up, owing to the indiscreet conduct of PETRAKOGEORGIS' gang over the Easter celebrating some weeks before.

Intensive enemy activity, patrols, etc. now began all along the South coast, prohibiting its use for evacuation purposes. It was the opinion of several BLOs [British Liaison Officers] that the GERMANS were expecting an invasion. After three days' fruitless waiting at AYIA PARASKEVI, I decided to push NW with my henchman to contact ISLD or [Captain Dick] BARNES [of Force 133, a cover-name for SOE] directly and use their sets for arranging the evacuation. MOSS remained behind with the General and the party and did splendid work keeping them cheerful and optimistic through these trying days. I had heard that one of the sets was at PANTANASA, but found it had pushed further West. I spent the next two days sending runners out in all directions till I finally contacted Capt. STOCKBRIDGE of ISLD and Capt. BARNES of Force 133. The latter contacted me at YENI on the 7th May.

On the morning of the 8th a runner brought a message, stating that Force 133 was sending in a SBS [Special Boat Service] party of [George] JELLICOE's with a W/T and instructions to contact us at all costs near LIMNI beach. This was most encouraging and showed the Office was doing the utmost to back us up a hundred percent, and would have been a solution to all our difficulties. Unfortunately hot on this runner's tail came another, whom I had sent to recce that particular beach, with the intelligence that Huns pullulated there and a post had been established as at SAKHTOURIA. So there was nothing for it but to move Westward to find a place where we could slip through the net.

Capt. MOSS and the main party meanwhile had advanced to PATSOS (MR: 625265) via YERAKARI (MR: 654240) where I contacted him, and on the night of the 9th/10th we marched to PHOTINOU, exchanging escorts on the way. On the night of the 10th/11th we marched on through VILANDREDO where I contacted Capt. CICLITIRA [SOE officer] who had moved to

ASI GONIA to meet us. We at once sent recce parties to a beach West of RODAKINO and suggested to Force 133 the night of the 14th/15th as a suitable evacuation date. Our scouts returned to state that the beach was miraculously free of Germans.

A W/T [message] came confirming our date, times, place and signals and on the night of the 13th/14th we struck south over the barren RODAKINO Mountains and reached the point at nightfall on the 14th.

MOSS gave the signals and the craft arrived on the stroke of 2300 hrs local time, as had been agreed. The first to land was Lieut. Bury and his Raiding Force, bitterly disappointed at missing the adventure of contacting us in the interior of CRETE. I repeat that the despatch of this raiding party was an excellent idea and might well have proved our salvation if things had been stickier.

The embarkation took place with model efficiency and dispatch and we set sail for MERSA MATRUH with our prisoner. It was a great relief for all of us to have brought the operation to a successful conclusion after these 18 anxious days in the CRETAN mountains.

The General's behaviour was most friendly and helpful throughout and he put up with the hardships of mountain travel and living rough with fortitude. MOSS and I had the impression that he had lost his nerve a bit after the first contact with us. He certainly made no attempt to escape.

One or two untoward events occurred. Firstly, the loss of his Knight's Cross of the Iron Cross on the first night's march, which we made every attempt to discover, and secondly, two very bad falls, one from a mule and another from a ten-foot precipice in the dark, in which he injured his shoulder. We surrounded him throughout with whatever amenities, i.e. mules, warm clothing, food, drink, bedding etc. that were possible in the circumstances, and he was treated both by ourselves and all our staff with all fitting deference and respect. I think he understood this and was grateful for it.

I should like to state that any credit to BRITISH Personnel for the success of this operation was due in exactly equal shares to Capt. MOSS and myself as we collaborated intimately on every single detail. The conduct and the backing of the CRETANS were superb. Our three main helpers in the abduction were: –

MANOLIS PATERAKIS, of KOUSTOYERAKO
GEORGE TYRAKIS, of PHOUPHOURA
MICHAEL AKOUMIANAKIS, of KNOSSOS

The rest of the abduction party, all old hands and worthy of praise, were: –

GREGORY CHNARAS, of THRAPSANO
Gendarme ANTHONY ZOIDAKIS, of AY YIANNI (AMARI)
ANTONY PAPALEONIDAS, of ASIA MINOR
Gendarme STRATIS SAVIOLAKIS, of ANAPOLIS
NIKOS KOMIS, of THRAPSANO
DIMITRI TZATZAS, of EPISKOPI (HERAKLION)
ELIAS ATHANASSAKIS, of HERAKLION
PAVLOS ZOGRAPHISTOS, of SKALANI

all representing different areas of CRETE.

TO THE GERMAN AUTHORITES IN CRETE

23 April 1944

Gentlemen,

Your Divisional-Commander KREIPE was captured a short time ago by a BRITISH Raiding Force under our command. By the time you read this he and we will be on our way to CAIRO.

We would like to point out most emphatically that this

operation has been carried out without the help of CRETANS or CRETAN Partisans, and the only guides used were serving soldiers of His Hellenic Majesty's Forces in the Middle East, who came with us.

Your General is an honourable prisoner of war, and will be treated with all the consideration owing to his rank.

Any reprisals against the local population will be wholly unwarranted and unjust.

Auf baldiges Wiedersehen!

.... Major
Commanding Raiding Force.

.... Capt.
Coldstream Guards.

P.S. We are very sorry to leave this motor-car behind.

Report No. 9

October to December 1944

After his long stint in hospital and another month on leave in Syria, Leigh Fermor finally returned to Crete in late October 1944. By then, the situation on the island had changed dramatically. Across the Eastern Mediterranean, German forces were withdrawing. Most of Crete was free. The enemy that remained – mostly Germans, but also a few thousand pro-Fascist Italians still loyal to Mussolini – had ensconced themselves in an enclave around Chania and seemed content to see out the war without excessive bloodshed, which, save for the occasional foray into guerrilla-held territory, they ultimately achieved. As he explains in the report, Leigh Fermor found one of those forays aimed at his own headquarters.

~

31 January 1945

I was again infiltrated into CRETE for the third time, arriving at AG GALENE on the Southern coast of CRETE, on the 28th October, 1944. I was met by Cpl LEWIS and left for HERAKLION the same night by jeep. The whole of CRETE was now freed except for the perimeter . . .

Arriving in HERAKLION I contacted Maj. RENDEL and Capt. HOUSEMAN. After spending three days in HERAKLION with the purpose of meeting the notabilities there in civil and military administration, I left for Western CRETE and the GERMAN perimeter . . .

It must be understood that this perimeter is enclosed by no defended line in the proper sense of the word but by a series of GERMAN strong points and agglomerations of troops. The Cretan line is also of the same nature with an ad hoc no man's land lying between them of anything from one to five miles. The GREEK positions are mainly along the line formed by [the] junction of the foot hills with the low lying country in the North of CANEA Province. The GERMAN perimeter of course contains the most important points in CRETE, i.e. CANEA town, the capital, SUDA BAY harbour and MALEME aerodrome . . .

The morale of the GERMAN troops was on the whole fairly high. They have ample supplies of food and overwhelming armament as all the field and anti-aircraft artillery and ammunition taken from the whole of CRETE had been accumulated in this comparatively small area. The predominant feeling among GERMAN troops seems to be that it is preferable for them to hold out as long as their food supplies last, relying either upon a change in the fortunes of war or a British invasion in force to which they would surrender. On no account will they surrender to Cretan irregular troops as they well know what fate will await them . . .

In the middle of November [*sic*: actually 8 December] the GERMANS launched an attack on my HQ in VAPHE consisting of seven tanks and about 400 infantry. They arrived at 0800 hours but were held up for half an hour by the road block which we had built two days before. When they reached the middle of the village the villagers all retreated to the heights surrounding the village and opened up on them with small-arms fire. During the day contingents from all the neighbouring villages arrived and attacked the GERMANS with such spirit that at about 1700 hours they were forced to retreat after having killed only four Cretans and destroyed only two houses. The GERMAN losses amounted to about thirty, including the Commandant of the VAMOS garrison, Capt. KELLER. This was considered by everybody to be a signal triumph for Cretan arms and an illustration of the almost unvarying success of the guerrilla tactics in guerrilla country against vastly outnumbering forces . . .

In the middle of December I moved from VAPHE to HERAKLION and remained there till I left the Island on 23 Dec. on board H.M.S. 'CATTERICK', reaching ALEXANDRIA on Xmas Eve.

My reasons for leaving the Island were that there was no real work for me to do and because I was anxious about missing the boat for SOE work in the Far East . . .

~

As stated in his report, Leigh Fermor left Crete in December 1944 with hopes of being posted to the Far East to fight the Japanese. Instead, SOE returned him to England and earmarked him for a new sub-unit called SAARF: the Special Allied Airborne Reconnaissance Force. This unit had been assigned the dangerous job of parachuting teams into Germany, beyond the reach of the advancing Allied armies, in an effort to secure the well-being of Allied prisoners of war. The target assigned to Leigh Fermor's team was the famous POW camp at Colditz. Ultimately, however, only one team was ever dispatched. Like other SAARF personnel, Leigh Fermor was assigned instead to catching war criminals as the Allies gradually seized control of Germany and Denmark. When the war ended, on 8 May 1945, he was in London. He was demobilised not long afterwards and returned to civilian life.

A GUIDE TO THE
ABDUCTION ROUTE

Chris and Peter White

A Guide to the Abduction Route

This guide is intended for your enjoyment, but beware: some of the sites are straightforward to find, whilst others take perseverance and effort – often requiring the use of GPS technology where the locations defy easy description. On these lesser-known routes you will need to follow shepherds' tracks, prepare for unproductive dead-ends, negotiate rough ground, spiny plants, fences and the occasional Cretan guard dog raving at the end of a rope. You will also need good walking boots, map and compass, water and sun protection. As the abduction party found, the mountain section over Psiloritis (Mount Ida) can get bad weather, including snow, up to late spring. Choose a fine day and turn back if the weather comes down.

The route can be followed on Google Earth using the coordinates given. These should be accurate to within 25m.

If **driving**, the locations are best reached by leaving your car on the nearest metalled road and then proceeding on foot. Though some sites have shepherds' tracks running close by, these are on private land, often gated, and may lead to terrain that is steep or impassable.

Buses are a good way to get to the start and finish of many of these routes. Information about bus times cane be found online.

Hitch-hiking in Crete is usually a successful way to get about – provided you are prepared for the occasional white-knuckle ride, sitting with the milk churns in the back of a shepherd's pick-up truck.

Maps are of variable usefulness. Best at the time of writing (2014) is the Anavasi 1:30,000 *Mount Idha (Psiloritis)* map which covers the route from north of Anogia into the Amari valley. The Anavasi 1:100,000 covers nearly the entire route before and after the abduction. Anavasi also publish a road atlas at 1:50,000 which is very useful. Other 1:100,000 maps in publication should be used with caution.

Parts of the route follow the E4 path across Crete. The E4 is one of the European long-distance paths. It starts in Spain, crosses Europe and visits Crete. It is marked – in Crete sometimes not very well – by yellow and black paint marks on pathside rocks, or by a yellow lozenge-shaped sign on a pole or tree (usually reduced to a sieve by target practice).

Routes of the journeys between the hideouts have been worked out using the descriptions in the texts and from information given to us by local Cretans. Where no strong evidence exists for the actual route, we have followed the most direct routes between locations using the paths and mule tracks that were in use at the time of the abduction. Some of these are now metalled roads or bulldozed shepherds' tracks. Interesting detours are suggested where there is some contemporary relevance.

Recommended reading

Antony Beevor, *Crete: The Battle and Resistance* (John Murray, 1991)

Sean Damer and Ian Fraser, *On the Run* (Penguin, 2006)

Xan Fielding, *Hide and Seek* (Secker & Warburg, 1955)

W. Stanley Moss, *Ill Met By Moonlight* (Harrap, 1950)

George Psychoundakis, translated by Patrick Leigh Fermor, *The Cretan Runner* (John Murray, 1955)

Oliver Rackham and Jennifer Moody, *The Making of the Cretan Landscape* (Manchester University Press, 1996)

The Heraklion Area

From Heraklion it is simple to follow the route taken from Archanes through to the Chania Gate. These locations are best explored with a car or by bus to Ano Archanes. Once in Heraklion it is simpler to follow the route on foot.

- **Kreipe's Headquarters, Ano Archanes**
  (35°14'19.03"N / 25°9'34.79"E)
- **Abduction Point** (35°15'51.69"N / 25°10'56.59"E)
- **Villa Ariadne, Knossos** (35°17'58.31"N / 25° 9'33.98"E)
- **Heraklion**
  - Gate of St George (35°20'16.22" / 25°8'9.94"E)
  - Morosini Fountain (35°20'20.59"N / 25°7'59.36"E)
  - Chania Gate (35°20'12.69"N / 25°7'29.53"E)

Kreipe's Headquarters in Ano Archanes is easy to find. Situated towards the N of the village on the main road between Ano Archanes and Kato Archanes, it is now a civic building and, if open, is well worth visiting for its atmosphere and wall paintings. This was the headquarters of the German Commander of the Heraklion sector of *Festung Kreta* – Fortress Crete. Kreipe left here at 21.30 hours on Wednesday 26 April 1944, planning to go back to his quarters at the Villa Ariadne for dinner.

The **Abduction Point** is 2km N of Archanes at the junction with the Heraklion road. From Heraklion take Route 99 towards Knossos; 5km past Knossos, just S of the village of Patsides, the junction appears on the right. A large modern memorial stands on the corner.

Some 500m back along the road to Archanes is a small outdoor museum, with military vehicles from the time of the Occupation including a Mercedes Benz saloon car, misleadingly labelled 'Kraipe [*sic*] 26-4-1943'. At the time of the abduction Kreipe's car was an Opel.

★

The party drove towards Heraklion, through Knossos and past the **Villa Ariadne**. The entrance to the villa is 300m from the main entrance to the Knossos excavations – situated on the left just before exiting the village on the way to Heraklion.

Built by Sir Arthur Evans in 1905 as his personal residence, the Villa Ariadne was gifted to the British School in Athens in 1926 for the use of the curator of the Knossos excavations. In the last week of April 1941 King George of Greece stayed here before his evacuation to Cairo on 30 April. The following month, during the Battle of Crete, it was used for a time as a field hospital by the British. After the Battle the villa became the headquarters of the Divisional Commander of the Heraklion Sector; Kreipe took up his post here in March 1944. On 9 May 1945 General Benthag was brought here from Chania to sign the unconditional surrender of the German forces remaining on the island.

From Knossos, to follow the route taken by the party through **Heraklion**, enter the Fortetza by the Gate of St George past Plateia Eleftherias, W along Dikeossinis to join Kalokerinou 50m S of the Morisini Fountain. Then head W for 800m to the Chania Gate.

THE POST-ABDUCTION ROUTE

It is possible to retrace the whole route taken by the abduction party from the village of Drosia (then *Yeni Gave*, where they continued their escape on foot) to Peristeres Beach on the S coast near Rodakino, where they were picked up by a British boat eighteen days later.

As a trek it will take seven to eight days, over the flank of the island's highest mountain, well away from the tourist trail and deep into the Cretan landscape and culture – the routes, in spring, passing through some of the finest wildflower landscapes in Europe.

ALTERNATIVE START

- **'Submarine Bay': Peristeres Bay** (35°24'20.38"N / 24°50'10.36"E)
- **Campo Doxaro** (*where the car was abandoned*) (35°20'48.13"N / 24°50'13.15"E)
- **Drosia/Yeni Gave** (*where they started the walk*) (35°20'34.58"N / 24°52'11.10"E)

By allowing an extra day, the route can be started on the north coast. Peristeres Bay is the location from which Leigh Fermor hoped the Germans would think the General had been spirited away by submarine. This enjoyable walk takes you up a beautiful valley from the sea, via the Vossakos monastery, to a road leading to Campo Doxaro where Leigh Fermor and George abandoned the car. It is then an easy walk along the road to Drosia where the party started their escape. This route offers the satisfaction of walking from coast to coast – Peristeres Bay to Peristeres Beach, sea to shining sea.

'Submarine Bay' to Drosia (via Campo Doxaro)
Peristeres Bay (annotated 'Submarine Bay' by Leigh Fermor on his map of the abduction route) is 7 km W of Sisses on the main Herakleion–Rethymno road. Buses will stop here if the drop-off is negotiated with the driver in advance. Keep an eye out for the landmarks of the bay to avoid missing it: Cape Peristeri and Peresteri island, and the two small islets in the bay close to the shore.

Leigh Fermor was fond of this bay: 'At the beginning of May [1943], I had 3 days leisure at Peristeri and spent most of the time bathing and made a recce of the promontory and Island on foot and swimming' (Report No. 3).

Dip your hands in the waters of the Aegean in anticipation of doing the same in the Libyan sea several hot and dusty days, and many miles, later. Cross the road and follow the valley S up the left-hand side of the dry streambed, along a track and old *kalderimi* (mule path) through olives and arbutus. The view back to the sea improves with height before the path crosses the valley to a sheep-fold, before tracking left and then right up the head of the valley. Take the new bulldozed track which leads steeply up left from the last leg of the zigzag to an agricultural building. Climb up behind this, through the pass, and descend 300m to the Vossakos monastery.

The *Monastery of Vossakos* is a beautiful and restful place in which to cool off in the shade and fill up with water.

Alternatively, the monastery can be reached by continuing on the zigzag track to a pass, through to a farm and cultivated area with a grove of fine ancient pines. Gain the metalled road 1km further on, turn left and walk N for 1km.

Take the road from the monastery S up to the watershed to be rewarded with your first views of Psiloritis (Mount Ida) in the distance. Consider that you will be climbing it in a few days' time. Descend the road to **Campo Doxaro** (where Leigh Fermor abandoned the General's car – minus its pennants) and walk 3.5km E along the 'old' Herakleion–Rethymno road to Drosia.

Main Route

- **North of Anogia** (35°18'36.20"N / 24°52'23.02"E)
- **Agios Fanourias/Petrodolakia/Nidha plateau** (35°12'45.98"N / 24°52'11.01"E)
- **North Hole** *'Vorini Trypa'* (35°10'38.12"N / 24°45'32.05"E)
- **Streambed/Agia Paraskevi** (35°08'54.38"N / 24°43'12.31"E)
- **Valley of Gomara/Agia Paraskevi** (35°9'12.83"N / 24°41'32.31"E)
- **The Kedros villages/Gerakari** (35°12'15.22"N / 24°36'36.87"E)
- **Patsos** (35°14'36.12"N / 24°34'53.10"E)
- **Photeinou** (35°16'12.22"N / 24°28'1.01"E)
- **Vilandredo** (35°16'11.35"N / 24°20'23.39"E;

35°16'14.50"N / 24°20'45.74"E; 35°14'48.00"N / 24°19'55.50"E)
- **Peristeres Beach** (35°10'58.36"N / 24°18'1.33"E)

Drosia to Anogia via the 'First Night caves'

Following the kidnap of General Kreipe late on the evening of 26 April 1944, Leigh Fermor and Moss with Manoli Paterakis, George Tyrakis and Strati Saviolakis, drive through Heraklion and out along the road to Rethymno. They stop just beyond Yeni Gave (now Drosia) and Moss, Manoli, Strati and the General head S down a track towards Anogia. Leigh Fermor and George drive on a further 3km to Campo Doxaro in order to dump the car and lay clues to indicate that the General has been taken to Peristeres beach and evacuated by submarine. They then travel through the night by a different path to Anogia.

On the W edge of Drosia, across the road from a chapel, an old path leads S to join the metalled road to the village of Aimonas. Walk S through the village and 2.5km along the road towards Livada, where a bridge crosses a small river. On the N side of the bridge – and 200m or so before it – a track runs E parallel to the river and heading into the river valley. Follow this track through the olive groves, negotiating fences, to follow the bank and eventually the bed of the river. After 1km the valley narrows into a gorge (35°18'42.46"N / 24°52'02.93"E).

The party spend the remains of the night and the following day – Thursday 27 April – in this valley and gorge. They are reunited with Leigh Fermor and George that evening on the outskirts of Anogia and depart heading S towards the Nidha plateau and Psiloritis.

The gorge is easily passable unless the river is in flood. You may get your feet wet in winter or early spring. There are many caves and potential hideouts along its sides. You eventually emerge into fields and on to a road/track that winds up S past a large shed to a junction with another track at some more sheds on the crest of the hill. Take the track E and then S towards Anogia.

There are several tavernas in Drosia, rooms in Theodora (the hamlet 500m W of Drosia) and a *kafeineon* in Aimonas. Note the water fountain in the centre of Drosia. There are many tavernas and places to stay in Anogia.

At *Damasta*, 3 miles E of Drosia and just to the W of the village, is a large memorial on a sharp bend in the road, commemorating a battle here on 8 August 1944. Moss, on his second mission to Crete, with a group of eight Andartes and six escaped Russian POWs, attacked and destroyed a detachment of over forty German and Italian troops and an armoured car on its way to attack Anogia.

Anogia to Nidha and the second hideout at Agios Fanourios/Petrodolakia

On the evening of 27 April 1944, the party reunites and begins the ascent of Psiloritis. They walk through the night, stopping for a brief rest at a cheese hut (mitado). They arrive eventually at the hideout of a band of Andartes led by Mihali Xylouris from Anogia. At the hideout three British SOE agents are waiting for them – John Lewis, John Houseman and W/T operator Reg Everson. They take several photos – published later in Ill Met By Moonlight. *(5°12'45.98"N / 24°52'11.01"E)*

One of the old droving paths from Anogia up to the Nidha plateau leaves from the bottom of the village, up past the chapel of Agios Nektarios and heads S, first on an old *kalderimi* through clumps of cistus and Jerusalem sage before joining a modern shepherds' track. The track winds SSW, through a striking floral landscape, Psiloritis looming closer at every turn. There are occasional short-cuts (on the old droving path) marked by E4 signs. Continue S at a junction in a wooded area passing a group of cheese huts and then the chapel of Agia Yakinthos (35°14'55.16"N / 24°51'43.45"E). About 300m past the chapel going E, strike off the path due S along the edge of a grazed area, to pick up another shepherds' track after 600m. Head S/SW on the track for just over 1km to a T-junction at a large prickly-oak tree. Walk S down the hillside behind the tree to the bottom of the valley and continue S up a slabby path to a lovely area, *Tria Yortho*, with a spring and water troughs.

Behind the spring is a shallow ravine that leads steeply up the hillside. Climb the slope on sheeptracks and remnants of an old *kalderimi* on the right-hand side of the ravine, past a craggy outcrop to a rocky plateau. Head S for 200m to pick up a shepherds' track and take this E for 2.5km until you approach the metalled road up to Nidha. To avoid some of the road walking, take a track that leads SW across the flank of the hill, 250m before the road, to pick it up again 750m further towards the plateau. After another 400m of tarmac, take the next metalled road which leads off left towards the University of Crete Observatory at Skinakas. After 600m you will see the church of *Agios Fanourias*. Opposite the church a shepherds' track leads off the road S towards the plateau. Walk 400m until you reach a small enclosed valley on the left with a shallow cave high up on the right. The features around and above the cave are still clearly recognisable from photographs taken at the time.

By car: take the road from Anogia up to the Nidha plateau. As you come to the plateau a metalled road leads off left towards the University of Crete Observatory at Skinakas. Take this road and after 600m you will see Agios Fanourios on your left. Park here and take the track that leads across the road from the church towards the Nidha plateau. You will find the small valley with the cave in it on the left after 400m.

At the Nidha plateau is a tavern with facilities for an overnight stay if negotiated in advance with the current owner (2014): good for an early morning start over the mountain. The owner also runs a taverna opposite the church on the *plateia* in Anogia's lower village. There are many tavernas and rooms in Anogia.

★

Agios Fanourios/Petrodolakia to the Amari Cave of 'Vorini Trypa' (35°10'38.12"N / 24°45'32.05"E)

The party arrive in the Amari valley in the early hours of Sunday 30 April, exhausted and cold after a difficult climb and descent over Psiloritis. They stay in the cave of Vorini Trypa for the day and light fires in order to dry their clothes. This marvellous cave, with its small entrance, gloomy interior with tunnels and chasms leading off, is well described in Ill Met By Moonlight. *(The cave also features as 'North Hole' in* The Cretan Runner *when used by Tom Dunbabin and George Psychoundakis in August 1944.) They leave the following night, heading towards Agia Paraskevi.*

The walk from the Nidha plateau over the flank of Psiloritis and down to the Amari is a major trek and the most arduous that the party took in their seventeen-day journey through Crete. Though not technically complicated, it requires an early start with a fine day forecast and plenty of water. Be prepared to cross some snow-fields until early summer. Map and compass are essential in case of bad visibility.

From the cave at Agios Fanourios head W and pick up a shallow valley heading down towards the plateau. Pass some shepherds' huts to come out on to the grassy floor of the plateau. Continue W across the plateau, enjoying the novelty of walking on soft, level ground, towards the taverna visible on the other side. Fill up with water at the taverna or at the Analipsis spring by the church up the hill behind. (There is none on the route.)

A photograph, not in general publication, shows the party climbing up the shallow gully a few metres W and below the start of the present E4 path, after visiting the *mitado* (cheese hut) of 'Roti'. The photograph 'Starting up the foothills of Ida' in *Ill Met By Moonlight* shows the party walking over some small walled fields – now mostly covered by the taverna car park.

From the taverna the track zigzags up to the Ideon Andron cave, legendary birthplace of Zeus. At the last bend of the zigzag, where the track returns N towards the cave, a clearly marked (yellow and black) E4 path climbs across and up the flank of the mountain to a valley which leads up W to the pass of Akolyta. Expect snowfields until late May.

From the ridge at the top of the valley, head down S to the flat bottom of this high level grazing area to pick up a shepherds' track. Follow this S to a junction and take the track W along a stony valley, under the looming grey cliffs of Mount Chabatha. Pass several old cheese huts and modern cisterns to the 'Gate of Ekdhora', where the path opens out on to the southern flank of the mountain. The views across the Amari valley to Mount Kedros, with the Libyan sea glistening to the S, are breathtaking. In the distant W the snowy peaks of the White Mountains massif float in the sky.

The path continues steeply down endless tiresome zigzags to the church of Agia Marina at the top of the Lochria roadhead. There is a spring and water troughs where the tarmac road ends – fill up here.

From here, as the crow flies, Vorini Trypa is only 1.7k due W, but navigation is not straightforward (GPS may be helpful). 100m W of the spring is a farm building. Walk in front of this and down into the sinkhole. From here cross this sinkhole heading W, up and over into another sinkhole. Cross this and head up its southern edge to pick up a track heading W and then S. After 600m this leads to the rim of a large fenced and cultivated sink-hole. Descend to the fence and follow it around anticlockwise. The small entrance to the cave of Vorini Trypa can be found below an old walled area up behind some oak trees on the N side of the sinkhole. Explore with care (torches required). The back of the cave is all void and abyss.

The path down to Nithavris starts from the opposite side of the sinkhole and leads to a junction after 250m. Take the down-ward track which winds W into the Amari valley past another circular sinkhole, walled around and across to divide it into two. (If you don't pass this distinctive sinkhole within 500m, you are on the wrong path.)

By car from the Amari valley, *either* approach from Agia Marina (via Lochria) following the directions for the walk (above) *or* park in Nithavris and ascend the mountainside on shepherds' tracks in a general E direction.

From Nithavris: As the crow flies, Vorini Trypa is 2.4km slightly N of E with an ascent of 500m from the *plateia* in Nithavris. After a few hundred yards you will pass a small church on your left – Panagia – located on a lower shepherds' track.

After the initial ascent a flatter area emerges, characterised by several cultivated sinkholes. Following the track that serves these sinkholes you will eventually come across a large, cultivated and fenced sinkhole. Follow the track down to this fence, then follow it around anticlockwise to the right. Vorini Trypa is tucked behind some rocks below a ruined sheepfold.

There is a small *kafeineon* in the centre of Nithavris and a larger taverna 200m further on towards the outskirts of the village, on the Apodoulou road. Rooms, shops, garage, *kafeineon* and a taverna can be found in Fourfouras.

Streambed/Agia Paraskevi (35°08'53.64"N / 24°43'12.25"E)
After leaving Vorini Trypa the party – at night and in miserable weather – slip through the German cordon and end up in an overgrown streambed near Agia Paraskevi where they spend a wretched and damp two days (1–2 May 1944).

From Nithavris walk down towards Agia Paraskevi on minor roads and shepherds' tracks through the olive groves. A streambed/ditch is found 1km SE outside Agia Paraskevi. The texts describe a streambed overgrown with cistus, thyme and myrtle – still growing there today.

Follow the field track on the left just after the small bridge 500m outside the village on the Agia Galini road. After 500m a shady streambed will be found on the left with a rocky outcrop below. A steep slope has recently (2014) been bulldozed below the outcrop.

★

Valley of Gomara/Agia Paraskevi (35°9'12.83"N / 24°41'32.31"E)
On the night of 2 May the party moves W of Agia Paraskevi to another location and stays there for seventy-two hours. The sun comes out and they are able to dry off. Both Moss and Leigh Fermor are vague about the location of this hideout. George Pharangoulitakis in Eagles of Mount Ida *is much more specific – siting it in the valley of Gomara, under a large pear tree and then in a grotto against a cliff.*

From the taverna in Agia Paraskevi walk W towards Agios Ioannis. After 1.6km a track bears off left into meadows and the Platis river valley. The area where the party hid appears on the left under a low cliff. Having explored the entrance to the gorge – you can swim – walk along the valley upstream until you come to the road.

At this point Leigh Fermor and George Tyrakis leave the General and the rest of the party in order to try and find a wireless set and establish contact with Cairo. They travel along the E edge of the Amari valley, heading initially to Fourfouras to stay with George's family there. The old mill and Turkish bridge – Manoura's Arch – under which George Psychoundakis hides in January 1943 (see The Cretan Runner*, 'The Germans are after me') can still be explored.*

By car: drive to the modern bridge between Agios Ioannis and Hordaki at the bottom of the valley. To reach the Gomara valley and gorge downstream, either follow the banks of the river or take an old overgrown path on the Agios Ioannis side of the river, accessed at the first bend in the road before the bridge. You come to meadows by the riverside with a low cliff on your left before the entrance to the gorge.

There is a *kafeineon* in Agia Paraskevi but nowhere to stay; a taverna and rooms may be found in Fourfouras. Agia Galini on the coast a few miles to the S has many tavernas and rooms, as does Agia Pavlos, further W, on the coast below Saktouria. Several arms landings took place here and Leigh Fermor was hoping to use this attractive beach for embarkation.

★

The Kedros villages and Gerakari

From Gomara continue W along the river bank and overgrown path to the road and modern and old bridges across the river. Climb the steep hillside towards Hordaki by road or on field tracks and follow the flowery lane through Ano Meros (tavernas) and the other Amari villages with their memorials. At the village of Vrises there is an old *kalderimi* leading up to Gourgouthi. Village rooms may be available in Ano Meros: ask in the *kafeineon*.

Gourgouthi (35°12'9.46"N / 24°37'31.63"E)
On the night of Friday 5 May the party – minus Leigh Fermor and George Tyrakis – walk through the tiny village of Gourgouthi on their way from the valley of Gomara to their next hideout above Gerakari. Walking through the village they peer in at a window and see the old men of the village distilling raki (described in Ill Met By Moonlight; *confirmed as Gourgouthi by Leigh Fermor). Gourgouthi sheltered several Allied soldiers in the springs and woods just behind the village after the Battle of Crete and also features in Xan Fielding's* Hide and Seek.

By car: take the signposted road just before Gerakari on the road from Ano Meros. On the Ano Meros–Gerakari road, close by the Gourgouthi turn-off, is the monastery of Agios Ioannis Theologos.

Hainospilia/Gerakari (35°12'15.22"N / 24°36'36.87"E)
The main party reach this sheepfold above Gerakari on the night of Friday 5 May 1944 and spend two nights here. Food is brought up to them from the village.

From Gourgouthi you can make your way up across the hillside to the sheepfold and cave of Hainospilia (1.3km, rough going). In spring, note the many different species of orchid which grow among the rocks. An easier path may be found by walking down to the main road and continuing to just outside Gerakari, where a shepherds' track, restored path and steps lead up the side of Mount Kedros to the cave and sheepfold. Commemorative signs are placed at the beginning of the track and beside the cave.

Taverna, hotel, rooms and a supermarket may be found in Gerakari.

The Eastern Amari detour

- **Fourfouras** (35°12'38.71"N / 24°42'43.35"E)
- **Pantanasa** (35°15'21.40"N / 24°35'37.21"E)
- **Genna** (35°15'4.72"N / 24°38'5.72"E)

George Tyrakis' House, Fourfouras (35°12'38.71"N / 24°42'43.35"E)

At the valley of Gomara Leigh Fermor and George Tyrakis leave the main party and head along the E side of the Amari in search of a working wireless set. They go first to Fourfouras and stay here on the night of 3 May 1944.

The house, currently in ruins, is on the road heading SW out of the village, 60m from the *plateia*. Note the remains of the mill on the inside. Taverna, *kafeineons*, minimarket, bakery, garage and rooms are all available in the village.

Pantanasa (35°15'21.40"N / 24°35'37.21"E)

Leigh Fermor and George Tyrakis leave Fourfouras and head to Pantanasa. They try to get information from local resistance leaders but initially meet with no success. Eventually credentials are confirmed and they are able to continue with their attempts to contact Cairo.

Genna (35°15'4.72"N / 24°38'5.72"E)

George and Leigh Fermor stay here – on the aloni *(threshing floor) of the goatherd Yourbovasili – for several days and nights while organising messages to and from the wireless station at Dryade, 26km to the WNW. George Psychoundakis is one of their messengers. They then travel on to rejoin the party at Patsos on 8 May.*

The circular floor of the *aloni*, clearly visible on Google Earth, can be found 100m below the Agia Fotini–Meronas road, 250m outside Agia Fotini.

Harakas sheepfold, Patsos (35°14'36.07"N / 24°34'57.04"E)

7 May 1944. Moss records that they had an easy night's march to Patsos and spent two nights here. Leigh Fermor and George rejoin them after their journey along the eastern side of the Amari in their search for a working wireless set. They rest and bathe in the stream below the hideout. A lamb is roasted and children help build the fire for it. George Pattakos from Patsos joins the party and leads the mule that the General uses for the next part of the journey. Kreipe watches as Leigh Fermor offers Evthymios Harocopos gold sovereigns for his efforts and support for the group, but the offer is refused.

From Gerakari take the road towards Spili. After 5km and at the brow of the hill, past a modern development on the left, take a shepherds' track on the N side of the road that runs back E then N through a gap between the hills. After the gap, take the tracks on the E side of the valley, through newly planted orchards and meadows down towards Patsos.

To find the hideout, take the track leading down towards a chapel, Agios Konstantinos, about 250m before the first farm of the village. After 250m on this track, go right on a path through a meadow and scrub. Harakas sheepfold is found in a wooded area on the right above the streambed and against an overhanging rockface. There is a commemorative sign in Greek. (GPS may be helpful.)

It is possible to clamber down into the streambed where Moss, in *Ill Met By Moonlight*, describes washing and falling.

By car: drive to Patsos and park by the taverna. Take the path that runs from between the taverna and the fountain up behind the village. Follow the track round to the E and 250m past a farm take the track that heads down left; then follow directions as above.

Photeinou/Olive Grove of Scholari (35°16'12.22"N / 24°28'1.01"E)

On 10 May the whole party – now reunited – walk from Patsos to Photeinou. They are now walking through less mountainous and more cultivated terrain. As they near Photeinou, Stavros Peros and his sons arrive to greet and escort them. Whilst at the olive grove Andoni and Despina Peros feed them – the newly-weds described in Ill Met By Moonlight.

Fill up with water at the fountain in Patsos. Leave the village heading W on the Karines road. At Karines, 5.5km, head N through the village to the metalled lane which winds on the S side of an open valley for 7km, to come out on the main Rethymno–Agia Galini road. Cross the road and walk N along the road for 500m and take the track leading off left into low hills. Pass between the hills, below the solar panel development and continue 1.5km N through an ancient cultivated valley. Before the village ahead and above, bear round W into a valley heading S to gain a track on the other side. The party stayed in the grove of old olive trees where a derelict stone hut is built against a large rock. (GPS is helpful.)

If approaching from Photeinou, find the entrance to a track 750m along the road heading S out of the village. Walk along the track back around the low hill for 500m until the olive grove appears on the right.

The closest tavernas are in Armeni or Spili (which also has rooms).

Photeinou contains the Venetian Fountain where Leigh Fermor met Kanaki Tsangarakis to explain the circumstances of his brother Yanni's death. Outside the village is 'Pavlo's cave' (see *The Cretan Runner*, 'At Photeinou') (35°16'12.68"N / 24°27'34.69"E).

Kato Poros Gorge/Vilandredo (35°16'12.63"N / 24°20'23.81"E; 35°16'8.56"N / 24°20'33.17"E; 35°4'48.00"N / 24°19'55.50"E)
After staying in Photeinou the party move through the night of Wednesday 10 May to Vilandredo, where they stay in three locations: they start in a built-up cave, where they meet with Dennis Ciclitira, high above the side of the gorge. They then move to a cave deeper into the gorge below them, then finally to a 'rocky and wooded fissure, an hour to the South'. The General falls again while climbing to this last hideout.

From Photeinou walk W out of the village below the low cliffs on to an old walled track leading over the rocky hill and down across the valley to Koumi. Walk through Koumi village and out the other side on to the metalled road that leads S towards Angouseliana. After 2.5km, after passing between two low hills, take a track leading W along the N side of a wide cultivated valley. Continue W, crossing into the head of another, wider valley and walk down to the road. Go S along the road for 300m, and take a track that leads along the S side of this wide valley. Crossing several shallow wooded watercourses the tracks lead W through an area known as Nifis Potamia for 5km, with higher ground on each side. Gain the metalled road and follow this 6.5km W through Velonado and on towards Vilandredo.

About 500m N after the Vilandredo village turn-off, on the road to Myriokefala, is a track on the right leading to a large sheep hut after 400m. Walk behind this and on to another smaller sheep hut 200m beyond. Climb the steep hillside directly above the hut to a wooded area and walled cave high on the hillside on the left. From here the party moved to another location further into the gorge. Unless the river is in spate, walk into the gorge along the streambed and after 1km the second cave appears up on the left side of the gorge.

The party then moved to a third hideout in the Vilandredo area (35°14'47.59"N / 24°19'53.70"E). This was the steep, rocky gorge that leads E up the side of Mount Krioneritis, 2km S of Vilandredo on the Vilandredo–Alones road. This point can be reached by old paths leading S out of Vilandredo or by road. The gorge entrance is just off the road on a sharp bend 100m before a sheep hut. The gorge itself is well worth exploring.

Moundros and Kato Poros gorges

A worthwhile detour can be made through the Moundros and Kolita/Kato Poros gorges via the abandoned village of Nisi. The gorges are cool and wooded, with dramatic narrowing cliffs and water-worn boulders, but are accessible and passable except when in winter flood (as George Psychoundakis and Xan Fielding discovered at Moundros in December 1942). Walking through the ruined houses of Nisi is a uniquely affecting experience – moving one to wonder how this once thriving community, with its fine houses and evidence of domestic and agricultural activity, should now be forsaken and derelict.

To reach the start of the walk take the track off the main road 700m N of Velonado, just past the bridge, which leads into the gorge. After 2.5km exit the gorge and bear E to come into Moundros village after 300m. There is a *kafeineon* on the main road. Continue N out of the village and 100m past the village springs take the track on the left leading down into the valley. Follow this across the river bed on to the other side of the valley. Continue W along the track for 1.5km to bear uphill into the ruins of Nisi.

Take time to explore this remarkable abandoned village, with its examples of *Kamara* house architecture – the traditional Cretan house, divided lengthways by a great arch (*kamara*) – laid bare to see. The external stairs, arches, sleeping ledges, kitchens, threshing floors, donkey mill and underground cisterns (look out for holes in the ground!) give a rare insight into life in rural Crete in earlier times. There are fine views N up the Kato Poros valley.

In October 1943, after the battle of Tsilivdika in the hills above Alones, George Psychoundakis brought the wife and children of Yanni Katsias from Kali Sykia to Nisi to stay with his aunt for safety. German and Italian units had received many casualties in the battle and general reprisals were feared in the area. A few days later the Germans went through Kali Sykia, Alones, Kallikratis and Rodakino burning and looting. Many villagers were massacred.

Continue S up the track out on to the stony ridge until you can zigzag W down to the valley floor and the entrance to the Kolita/ Kato Poros gorge. The cave the party used as their second location in the Vilandredo area will be found up on the W side of the gorge, with rough steps and a handrail leading to it. A feature of this gorge is the fine old plane trees that grow here, clinging to the boulders on the river bed. At the exit to the gorge, bear E and take the signposted path which leads to the road. The start point at Velonado is 1.5km E.

Nearest villages with tavernas are Argiroupoli (rooms) and Myriokefala. These last two villages are well worth exploring in their own right.

Peristeres Beach (35°10'58.36"N / 24°18'1.33"E)

On the night of 13 May the party hear that a boat is coming next evening. The party split again to cross the mountains. Leigh Fermor, Manoli Paterakis and the General take a more westerly route on which, owing to its isolation, they can travel by day, climbing the steep, difficult and trackless face of the mountain to the pass W of Krioneritis summit and then SSW down the spur towards Ano Rodakino. Moss and the others take a direct route walking through the night. They meet again the next afternoon on an outcrop above Ano Rodakino. During the afternoon of Sunday 14 May, the reunited party – now reinforced by many Andartes from Rodakino – make their way down to Peristeres beach.

There are few ways up the northern slopes of Krioneritis – the range that dominates the SW aspect of the valley. All are rough, steep and isolated and should only be taken by fit and prepared parties. Just one path is waymarked. This is the route taken by Moss and the main party.

From Vilandredo walk 5km along the road to Alones and take the marked E4 path up the hillside from behind the village hall. The black and yellow paint marks on the rocks are sparse and easy to miss. Make sure you have identified the next mark before leaving the last. Climb S up the steep, rocky hillside (rough going, with no clear path). When the gradient flattens off follow the ridge and signs W for 500m to a break in the ridge and a view down to the Rodakino villages and Libyan sea. The views from the top of the ridge are extensive and dramatic. In spring, the crest is covered with hundreds of yellow asphodels. A shepherds' track should lie directly below you. Scramble steeply to the track which zigzags down the mountain. Trend W after the first shepherds' hut to come into Kato Rodakino.

Tracks lead down SSW, across the road and down to Peristeres beach. Note the stream that runs down to the sea – referred to in *Ill Met By Moonlight*, where they find an old man tending his garden.

By car: Walk to the beach along a coastal track that follows the shore from Polirizos beach – reached from Rodakino by taking the road down to Korakas and then driving 1km W to the end of the coast road.

There are a number of tavernas and rooms along the coast road from Korakas beach to Polirizos beach. At the time of writing, the owner of the Korakas Beach taverna and apartments is Vardis Hobitis, grandson of the Rodakiniot Andarte leader, Vardis Hobitis, who had his house burnt down twice by the Germans. Vardis is very knowledgeable about the history of the local Andarte group and speaks good English.

At 10 p.m. on 14 May 1944, ML 842, captained by Brian Coleman and with a unit of commandos, arrives and evacuates Leigh Fermor and his party from the island. They leave their boots on the beach and sail for Egypt and safety.

NOTE

This guide could never have been made without the generosity, advice and encouragement given to the authors by the Cretan people living in the villages along the route. Their interest and pride in sharing their history with us has been a wonderful experience for which we both remain enormously grateful.

A Note on the Contributors

Roderick Bailey is a historian of irregular warfare and a specialist in the study of Britain's Special Operations Executive. His books include the acclaimed official history of SOE's war on Fascist Italy, *Target: Italy – The Secret War Against Mussolini*. A graduate of Cambridge and Edinburgh Universities, he has also served in Afghanistan with the British Army. He is currently a Wellcome Trust research fellow at Oxford University.

Chris and Peter White have walked the Kreipe abduction route on several occasions and, with the help of local Cretans, they have researched, found and recorded many of the exact locations used by SOE and the Cretan Resistance.

Acknowledgements

The publishers and contributors would like to express their gratitude to David McClay and Graham Stewart of the National Library of Scotland for their kind assistance with access to documents, manuscripts and photographs from the Sir Patrick Leigh Fermor Archive. They would also like to thank John Benning and Daniel Dendy for their perseverance in typing the reports.

Illustration Credits

INDEX